QUAINT WE AIN'T

QUAINT WE AIN'T

A country editor confesses the hilarious truth about life in small towns.

by J. Tom Graham

NEW WIN PUBLISHING, INC.

Copyright © 1994 by J. Tom Graham

All rights reserved. No part of this book may be used or reproduced in any manner whatsoever without prior written permission from the publisher except in the case of brief quotations embodied in critical reviews and articles. All inquiries should be addressed to:
NEW WIN PUBLISHING, INC., P.O. Box 5159, Clinton, NJ 08809

Library of Congress Cataloging-in-Publication Data

Graham, J. Tom, 1942–
   Quaint we ain't : a country editor confesses the hilarious truth about life in small towns / by J. Tom Graham.
   p. cm.
   ISBN 0-8329-0511-9 : $17.95
   1. Country life—United States. 2. Villages—United States. 3. Graham, J. Tom, 1942– . 4. Newspaper editors—United States—Biography. I. Title.
GT3470.G73 1994
307.76'2'0973—dc20   94-37807
                                                                               CIP

TABLE OF CONTENTS

Foreword	vii
What They Fail to Teach in Journalism School	1
Kathryn and the Exploding Biscuit Cans	9
An Ovation at the Alcalde	13
Thirteen Pigs and Haute Cuisine	21
The Stomping Savior of the Tent Revival	29
The Night the UFO Landed in the Front Yard	39
Horsefeathers and the Virgin Mary	43
Cows Have No Respect for Science	51
The Feel of Hair-Face Stubble on Spain's Hottest Hand	57
The Secret Wisdom of the Secret Ballot	67
Reggie the Rock Critic	77
Why I Gave Up Sportswriting as a Career	83
Judge Al and the Change of Venue	89
The Balloon Lady of Dublin	99
The Star of the Police Scanner	105
Spinning a Yarn, Spinning a Truth	111
Inventing the Cucumtaloupe	121
The Night I Didn't Spend in the Red Light District	125
Faith and the Flashbulb	135
Poisoning in Papa Doc's Paradise	139
A Little Advice at Thirty	149

FOREWORD

His huge wrinkled hands threw the metropolitan newspaper down on the coffee-drinking table at Kitchen's Hardware.

"Why, whenever a big city newspaper or television reporter does a story about any small town, does the reporter always call us 'quaint'?" the septuagenarian named Neal demanded to know. "They cannot do one single story without saying something about our 'quaint people' or our 'quaint shops.' You're supposed to be a newspaperman, Graham. You tell me why your colleagues in the fourth or fifth or whatever unreal estate they consider themselves always label us as 'quaint.' "

Neal was an old geezer, a certified paper-carrying old geezer who had labored for years to be worthy of that lofty title, and any experience-scarred country editor knows better than to argue with someone who has risen to the status of old geezer. So I tentatively replied, "I don't know, Neal, but don't you think the word 'quaint' has a nice connotation to it? It implies something charming, perhaps a bit old-fashioned, but charming nonetheless."

"Charming my arse," Neal said. Old geezers are allowed to talk like that. "Quaint means something strange. It means something that is not quite right, something strange or curious."

"I suppose the big city folks do consider us a bit curious or foreign," I said. "Is that so bad?"

Neal picked up the newspaper section and hurled it again: "We are the ones who are 'strange'? Have you ever been to one of their damn cities? They could call us old-fashioned. They could call us 'kooks' or whatever else they want. But quaint we ain't."

WHAT THEY FAIL TO TEACH IN JOURNALISM SCHOOL

At eight o'clock on a Monday morning, I walked into *The Inquirer* as its new editor with my journalism degree under my arm and fully prepared to teach this historic southern newspaper how to join the 20th Century.
I had no concept of how much I was to learn.
The Inquirer was a daily newspaper located a half block off the town's two squares. Just inside the front door clacked the Associated Press teletype machine producing reams of paper about the vital news of the world. But the newsroom was nowhere in sight. All I could see were rows of pencils, adding-machine tape, and other office supplies.
I wandered toward the back of the long and narrow building and introduced myself to Bud, the business manager of *The Inquirer* operations. He pointed me to a small office area in the extreme rear of the building where there were four desks. Two were for the advertising department, and two belonged to the editorial department, over which I had been hired to preside.
I met Mrs. Jo, a woman in her late 60s who was the society editor and my only staffer. She worked part-time. A gracious but reserved woman, she was typical of the people in the German belt. She imparted no information without being directly asked and even then as little as required.
"Where is the editor's desk?" I asked.

"This one," she said, motioning to one tucked away behind Bud's filing cabinets, yet facing her own.

Before I could sit down at the desk, old man Ed came in the front door. Ed was the publisher of *The Inquirer*, a family newspaper for decades. It had been Ed who hired me, and I expected to receive some modest amount of instruction from him. But I was wrong. His brother, Henry II, had been the newspaperman. Ed had been forced to step in after Henry II died suddenly of a heart attack. Ed was a rancher who spent his days sitting at the Alcalde Hotel's coffee shop, and he was already late for the morning debate certain to be well underway.

"Henry will show you around," Ed said, and he departed.

Henry was Henry III, the son of the former publisher and the grandson of the founder. Henry III was, as it turned out, advertising director of *The Inquirer*, but his heart was in the real estate business.

I attempted a few questions the editor of a daily newspaper needs to know:

"How many pages do we have today?"

"Eight," said Mrs. Jo.

"Do we have any news to go in them?"

Before Mrs. Jo could give me another one-word answer, Henry III came strolling in. He had a warm smile and handshake and seemed genuinely glad to see a new editor on board. He would take me around the town and introduce me to everyone beginning at that moment.

I followed Henry III back through the skinny building while he explained that *The Inquirer* was a four-thousand circulation, six-day daily newspaper. It was also a weekly newspaper, an office supply shop, a commercial printing establishment, and it did office equipment repair and commercial photography on the side.

"That is everything," I thought to myself, "a small-town newspaper can do to make a few bucks.' But none of this concerned me. I had grown up as a printer at a weekly newspaper. I had worked my way through the university while working at the town's daily newspaper, first as a printer and then as a reporter. When I graduated from college, I had been promoted to city editor. I could easily handle anything the little *Inquirer* had to throw at me.

Henry III walked out onto the worn old streets with me in tow. Here is a town, I thought, which has a comfortable Deep South feel. Henry introduced me to the merchants, to the folks in the century-old courthouse, to the people in city hall, to everyone all morning long. As lunch approached, he took me to the Alcalde Hotel where coffee was still a nickel, even in the 1960s, and where the plate lunch special was still Depression Era priced.

About one-thirty, Henry departed for his after-lunch nap, and I walked back over to the newspaper. I thought that the afternoon daily must already be on the press, and I was more than passively interested to see what we had printed that day.

To my surprise, I found Eric, the newspaper's production manager, standing beside the editor's desk patting his foot with impatience. Upon my arrival back in the newsroom, Mrs. Jo cocked her head with stern disapproval.

"Where have you been?" she wanted to know.

"Time it is for *The Inquirer* to go to press," Eric told me in a thick German accent. "Ve have no stories; ve have no dummies (page layouts); ve have nothing."

I was frozen with fright. I had just spent four college years working for an afternoon daily, and if it wasn't on the streets being delivered by one in the afternoon, every employee's job was in peril.

"You mean, nothing's been done?" I asked incredulously.

"You are the editor," Mrs. Jo correctly pointed out. "We have been awaiting your instructions."

I had never even sat down at my desk. I didn't even

know where the pencil sharpener was located. Now I had to produce the newspaper instantly, a full day's work in minutes. Sweat broke out on my brow as I ripped into the Associated Press copy and instructed Eric just to run the national and state budget stories. We would go with them, whatever they might be. As I attacked the piles of paper on my desk, Eric disappeared.

I looked through the pile of mail and picked a couple of local things that I thought might be appropriate on the front page, and with only a glance for an edit, I wrote headlines on them. I dashed off headlines on the wire stories from the budget summaries as rapidly as I could. Soon I had a pile of stories and headlines that needed to go to typesetting . . . and fast.

I leaped up from my desk and looked around.

"Where is production?" I asked.

Mrs. Jo looked up from her desk and responded only to the question I had asked. "It is in the building next door."

"If I want to go there, how do I do it?"

"You can go out the front door to this building."

So I scooped up an armload of stories and headlines and headed through the long building past the office supplies, the AP machine and out the front door onto the sidewalk. Then I turned up the street to the entrance of the next building, also a long and skinny one, and went inside past the office supply shop and the photography department into the back where newspaper production was located. I shoved the headlines and stories to Eric, who sorted them between the two linotype operators.

Then I dashed back through the long production building, out onto the sidewalk, back into the first building to my desk. The whole thing was a distance of some 250 feet, and after I had made several trips like that, I was winded and weary. I looked again to Mrs. Jo.

"There must be some way," I pleaded, "to get this copy into production without having to run out onto the sidewalk."

With a sort of "why didn't you ask" smile, she pointed to the rear of the building. "You can throw them down the evaporative air-conditioning chute."

"I can what?"

"You can stand up on those Coke cases and throw the copy down the air-conditioning vent. It goes right into the back of production."

"Oh," I said. With eight pages to be produced, I had no time to argue. I ripped the paper out of my typewriter, went over to the stack of four Coke cases, climbed on top, reached up into the sheet metal air-conditioning vent and let them fly. Flutter . . . flutter . . . flop.

"No, no, no," Mrs. Jo said as she watched from her desk. "You have to throw them around a turn in the chute. Stand up on your tiptoes, and throw them around that corner."

I pulled the paper out of the chute, drew back my best pitching arm, and hurled what I hoped would be a curve around the corner which was a couple of feet inside the chute. Flutter . . . flutter . . . flop.

"No, no, no," Mrs. Jo said. She shook her head as if they had taught me nothing those four years in journalism school. "To go around that corner, the paper has to have some body to it. Wad it up a little."

"You want me to wad up this story I just rewrote?"

"Just a little . . . so it can make it to the bottom of the air conditioning chute."

I folded the paper rather carefully and tried again. It went around the corner, but . . . flutter . . . flutter . . . flop.

"No, no, no," said Mrs. Jo as she got up from her desk and went to the corner for a long push broom. "You have to make a kind of ball out of it." She took that broom, climbed atop the Coke cases, and swabbed the air-conditioning vent with the broom so any copy stuck in it would be pushed to production in the adjoining building. Then she took one of her own stories and showed me how it was done. She crumpled that wedding story into a ball, and with a Carl Hubbell movement which defied her 60-plus years, she adroitly hurled that story into the air-conditioning chute and around the corner.

"Like that," she said. "Only not too hard. If the paper has too much velocity once it reaches the bottom of the chute, it keeps going and gets sucked into that fan by the linotype machine. Turns it into confetti."

I was stunned. This was obviously an acquired skill, but if *The Inquirer* was to have an issue that day, I would have to practice as I went along. I typed a couple more headlines, tore them out of the typewriter, rolled them into loose balls of paper, and hurled them into the air-conditioning chute as hard as I could. Flutter . . . flop. The broom was needed to swab them down.

But soon I was wadding and pitching to the backshop without throwing too many bloopers, and progress was at least being made. It was more like throwing a slider, I decided, than attempting an actual curve ball.

Before *The Inquirer* hit the streets that afternoon, the time was almost four o'clock, more than two hours late, and everyone in the building looked at me with some degree of displeasure. There were doubts that this new editor was going to work out. What had he been learning in that college anyway?

When the last carrier had finally departed with his rolled bundle of newspapers, I trudged to my rented room and collapsed, punished but not beaten. Tomorrow, I vowed, would be different.

The key to producing an afternoon daily, especially when there is a two-person staff, is to get an early start, I decided. So I got up at four in the morning on the following day, and I walked through a heavy rain to *The Inquirer* office.

Before five o'clock, I was pulling the wire copy, ripping it, writing headlines. Then I would wad it up and throw it down the air-conditioning chute. Then I wrote local stories from information people had submitted. I wadded these stories up and hurled them into the air conditioning. By the time the rest of the newspaper's employees arrived at eight o'clock, I would have the Tuesday edition of *The Inquirer* under control, perhaps even almost ready for make-up.

But instead of the approving nods that I had expected when the production department arrived, I saw Eric coming at me in anger. He held up soaking wet stories and headlines which he had collected from the bottom of the air-conditioning vent.

"No, no, no, you didn't," said Mrs. Jo with her sternest "will he ever learn" expression. "You cannot throw the stories down the vent when it rains. Water collects at the bottom, and everything gets soaked."

"Will I have to start over?" I said with eyes as moist as the headlines dripping in front of me.

So pathetic was my appearance that Eric and Mrs. Jo both laughed a little, a lot I later learned by German-belt standards.

"No," Eric said. "Ve dry de stories on de lineclothes between de linotypes. Maybe okay dey be."

The Inquirer went to press that Tuesday on time, and I began to understand how much I had to learn in the German belt before I could truly be called its editor.

KATHRYN AND THE EXPLODING BISCUIT CANS

Anyone who has ever owned a small business knows how hard it is to employ a good bookkeeper.

The task is doubly difficult in the weekly newspaper business because of the low wages and the high volume of tiny classified and circulation transactions which must be painstakingly tracked.

So after years of trying, I gave up on being able to retain a bookkeeper on salary. In desperation, I broke down and married one.

Her name is Kathryn, and I must admit that the arrangement has been, for the most part, quite satisfactory. The books at the newspaper have been a model of accuracy, and I am unafraid of inspection by any crack team of postal or internal revenue auditors. The marriage contract is much stronger than an employment one, and this makes it unlikely she will change positions for another ten dollars a week. Her attention to detail and determination to locate that missing dime from the cash box more than offsets my "close is good enough" approach.

But to balance all of these assets, one might expect a liability or two.

Kathryn comes complete with an assortment of quirks, one of which really gives me a "rise."

Psychologists have a name for just about every kind of phobia it is possible for a human being to display, but what would they call someone who is deathly afraid of pop-open biscuit packages? Is that fear called "doughbia"? Or is it "Pillsburyobia"? Fortunately, I am not charged with naming this phobia. It is tough enough just to describe it.

You see, Kathryn has this little problem with those refrigerated biscuit cans in the grocery store. They "explode," and the prospect of that almost scares her blind.

Well, they don't actually "explode." At worst, they sort of "pop" open — if you're lucky.

But to Kathryn, the anticipation of that little "whoosh" is more than she can stand.

I have known for many years that she was frightened of biscuit packages. On those rare occasions when she decided to cook me breakfast, she always made me get the biscuits from the icebox and open them while she backed way, way off — sometimes into the adjoining room.

Usually, my only emotion towards the package of biscuits is one of aggravation because it will not open easily enough. I peel off the paper wrapping, mash at the seam with my finger, and yet it still holds. I have to grab a spoon and punch a hole in it before the little "pop" occurs which allows one to get at the dough. Sometimes, I bang it against the kitchen counter with a hunter-provider instinct normally suppressed by prepackaged food.

However, Kathryn is just the opposite. She is worried almost to total distraction that the little biscuit can might "go off" in her hand. The fact is that even if it "exploded" right under her nose it would hurt absolutely nothing. Intellectually, she knows this and can discuss it almost rationally. But this reasoned understanding is of little value when overridden by her phobia.

It is not knowing when the little biscuit can will pop open that is her torture.

After fifteen years of partnership in business and life, Kathryn's phobia finally reached such an intensity that she brought the subject up for conversation.

"Do you wonder why we never have biscuits?" Kathryn asked.

"Because you are afraid to open the packages," I correctly surmised.

"It's worse than that," she confessed. "I am afraid even to touch them in the grocery store. I don't like to stand next to them in the biscuit cooler. In fact, I am even afraid to push my cart down the aisle the biscuits are on."

"But Kathryn," I responded, "don't you think that is a bit obsessive? Thousands of people push their carts past stacks of biscuit packages every day, and as far as I know, there has never been a fatality."

"Joke if you must," she said, "but let me tell you the process I went through this week to buy one package of them. I had to make three passes down the dairy aisle before I could bring myself to go near them. I stopped my grocery cart more than ten feet away. I opened my purse and pulled out a pair of tongs I had brought just for the occasion.

"Cautiously and with my arms extended to full length, I crouched and approached the biscuits."

Unfortunately, she related, a crowd began to gather and watch, so she was forced to put the tongs back in her purse and go around the aisles another two or three times until that particular part of the grocery store was empty.

Then she removed the tongs, extended her arms, and sidled up to the biscuit counter. With the tongs, she gripped the top package of biscuits, lifted it carefully into the air, and slowly eased it into a medium plastic sandwich bag which she had prepared to contain the blast, should one occur. Once zipped, the plastic bag went into the far front corner of the grocery cart. She could not have been more careful if she were a combat engineer disarming a tank mine. She ignored the laughter of a man who had pushed his cart up behind hers.

All the way home from the store, she worried about the

biscuits being in the trunk of her car, and she could not relax until she had placed the plastic grocery bag into the refrigerator and, using the tongs, had slipped the sandwich bag containing the package of biscuits into a secure position in the vegetable bin. Bomb squads should work with such precision.

"My phobia about those biscuits is getting worse," she confided to me needlessly. "What am I going to do?"

"Why don't you make biscuits from scratch like mother used to do?" I asked with the most constructive of intentions.

"Get real," she shot back.

There we were at an impasse. I like biscuits, but it worries Kathryn to have such a volatile substance in her kitchen, even behind the reinforced doors of a General Electric.

It was obvious the biscuits had to go. I can always get a biscuit down at the El Norte Cafe, but heaven knows where I'd ever find another bookkeeper.

AN OVATION AT THE ALCALDE

Nothing hinders a journalist more than catching a virus of idealism and having to fight the pernicious intruder off.

Unfortunately, most of us journalists who were college-exposed in the convulsive 1960s were not only carriers but also infectors of the various true-believer diseases.

While my cohorts were sitting around in marijuana-souped garage attics waiting for the "revolution" to come which would end all war and make lovers of everyone, I packed my state university idealism into a knapsack and headed for the front lines of the civil rights movement: A small southern town which was just sitting there minding its own business and trying not to notice that the 20th Century had arrived six decades ago. The historical traditions were the by-laws of the town, and the keeper of these traditions were the Daughters of the Republic, the most powerful organization in the county.

I was editor of *The Inquirer*, a newspaper which had not inquired about anything in living memory, but I took my new position as the purveyor of truth and justice to this closed community as seriously as any zealot.

My newspaper would treat the races equally. (Fortunately for me, I had no politically correct concept in those days that the sexes had to be dealt with equally as well, or I would never have survived.)

I had some idea that this might grate upon the slow-paced deliberations which took place every morning in the nickel coffee shop of the Alcalde Hotel where the great minds of the town gathered to consider the issues of the day. After the Daughters, this was the second most powerful gathering in the community.

The Alcalde perched its anachronistic self only a couple of main street doors down from the newspaper office, and I noticed right away that there was something almost sacred about Publisher Ed's morning treks down to the place.

When Ed said, "I'm going down to the Alcalde," everyone in *The Inquirer* understood that he was not to be disturbed by trivial issues such as catastrophes or Second Comings. He was doing his publisher's thing with the townsfolk. Even more tense was the one day a year when he "settled up" with the owner of the Alcalde. For the past 12 months, no money had changed hands between them, but on this one day of the year, Ed would gather up all of the Alcalde's purchases at the newspaper and take them down to the Alcalde, where the owner would tally a year's worth of Ed's coffee and daily lunches. The one who ended up owing the other money would pout about it for a week or so.

After I had been at the newspaper for several turbulent months, Ed invited me to go with him to the Alcalde coffee shop. I recognized this as some kind of tentative honor.

The Alcalde was a hotel which still rented fan-cooled rooms, and its large open lobby had a tropical feel to it which could have inspired Somerset Maugham. A screen door separated the lobby from the coffee shop with its restaurant seating hidden in back as if one had to be invited before one could indulge in the plate lunch specials.

The instant Ed's foot poked through the screen door and came down on the coffee shop floor, the publisher began to be harangued by the local version of the Algonquin debating society. Especially vociferous was the owner of the Alcalde, an Arab-American who stalked the counter and put down John Birch sophisms with every cup of coffee. The wall behind him was still papered with Goldwater for President posters as a matter of loser's pride, although he would quickly tell you that the Arizona senator was far too liberal for Alcalde tastes. The hotel owner looked at me, the tag-along-behind new editor, with one squinted eye and one large suspicious one.

"I see you brought your nigger editor with you," the hotel owner blurted out to the publisher.

Nigger editor? His comment was so rude and unexpected that my brain required a couple of seconds to process this insult. I wasn't black. But I quickly realized it was my change in policy which allowed photographs of Negroes to appear in *The Inquirer* which had caused him to hang that epithet on me. My mind stammered for something to say in retort while I trailed behind the unphased Ed as he sat down at the counter just as nonchalantly as if the Alcalde owner had smiled and said "good morning" instead.

"Yeah," Ed said as he accepted both the friendly cup of coffee and the unfriendly greeting with equal aplomb, "I brought my nigger editor . . . and my white editor as well. I can only afford one editor, and he has to be editor for everyone."

Before I arrived, *The Inquirer* had never run a photograph of a black who was not charged with murder, rape, or some other felonious crime.

A man I recognized as one of the county's biggest chicken farmers spoke up from a table behind me: "I'll tell you one damn thing. You won't run a bridal picture of my daughter on the same page as you run some nigger's wedding."

"I don't think we have to worry about that, Aaron," said Ed as he poured two heaping spoons of sugar into his cup and stirred as casually as if the discussion topic were the weather. "As I recall, your daughter got pregnant and ran off with that Mexican boy. I don't think we ever got a bridal picture of her down at *The Inquirer*, did we Aaron?"

Thompson, the feed store owner, launched a comment from the far end of the room: "I never thought I'd live to see the day when the football team at the nigger high school got a picture and story same as our Bulldogs."

Ed was unflappable: "At least the nigger team is winning. Hell, Thompson, they're ranked second in the state among the Negro schools."

The owner of the Alcalde leaned over his counter and stared the publisher straight in the eye with the question that was on everyone's mind: "Ed, when are you going to fire this nigger lover and bring in somebody else to edit your newspaper?"

"Well, I'll tell you fellas what," Ed said pausing to sip on his coffee. "You find me another editor who is college educated, able to read and write, willing to live in this little town, and willing to work seven days, 60 or 70 hours, for $110 a week, and I'll fire this one."

The coffee shop fell silent for a dead-air minute; then Ed stood up and said he had to go look after an old sick cow as if the conversation had dealt with nothing else. I followed him out of the Alcalde with sudden respect for this little short man. It's one thing to march in a Washington, D.C., protest and argue with bigot strangers; it's quite another to sit down among life-long friends and absorb their arrows without flinching.

But as I reflected on that morning, I came to understand that Ed took me with him for a reason. He wasn't trying to rub the noses of the Alcalde crowd in the new realities of the mid-1960s. Instead, the trip was for me. He wanted his idealistically clad young editor, who could distinguish only the extremes of black and white, to experience the grays of a long-settled little town. Perhaps the Alcalde coffee shop was his way of letting me know that he agreed with what I was doing but he also wanted to make certain I understood the realities of how the town was reacting. I think it was his way of teaching me not to back people into a corner where they had to fight. Make sure they have plenty of elbow room to turn the other direction when the time is right.

"You never win today's argument," Ed used to say. "The way you can tell if you won yesterday's argument is if your opponent changes his viewpoint over to yours the next time the subject comes up."

And sure enough, the "elbow room to turn a little" proved valuable a short time later. As the new guy in town, I was made chairman of the Chicken Festival Parade, quite a privilege I thought for about 15 minutes. Then I came to understand that everyone else in town knew better than to be chairman of the Chicken Festival Parade. The Daughters of the Republic dictated everything for this traditional festival from the wreath laying at the cemetery to the crowning of the Chicken Festival queen. They expected the parade to be just as perfect.

As parade chairman, I was summoned to a festival steering committee meeting of the Daughters of the Republic and given an absolute route that the parade had always followed and an inviolate order by which the parade entries must proceed. That was fine with me. I had no inclination to alter either the parade route or order. I only wanted to survive this additional community duty.

But the plan for the parade soon got off on the wrong foot, perhaps because I was parade chairman. A group of blacks in the community came to me and entered a float for Mount Zion Baptist Church. Sitting atop the float would be the long-time minister of the church who was to be honored for his half century of service to the cloth. I gladly accepted this parade entry without the slightest premonition that I was covering myself in faux pas.

Only when the festival chairman for the Daughters of the Republic angrily telephoned me and demanded to know what I had been thinking did I begin to understand. A Negro float had never been entered in the Chicken Festival

Parade. After all, she informed me, those people had their own Juneteenth celebration. Their floats went in that parade. (For non-Texans, Juneteenth is June 19th, the day when Texas slaves learned that they had been freed by Abraham Lincoln's Emancipation Proclamation.)

However, the black leaders had watched Martin Luther King carefully and had learned to be on solid moral ground before making a stand. The blacks had selected a man to be honored who was universally admired. Even the Alcalde coffee group debaters respected this man. His wife and sisters had been their nannies. They had watched this old gentleman work full-time in the fields and preach full-time in the churches as he took care of his people without complaint and without asking for help. It was morally right that his 50th year in the ministry be recognized by a float in the parade.

So as the day of the parade arrived, an undercurrent of turmoil flowed through the streets. The Daughters of the Republic continued to demand that I disqualify the black parade entry, but I had already accepted that float, and I had no intention of scratching it. Instead, I positioned the black float in the place of honor behind the Bulldog High School Band, and I wrote a very harsh editorial condemning the Daughters for pointlessly disrupting the festival. To my surprise, Ed let the editorial go into print.

I swear what happened next was an accident stemming from the incompetence of youth, but the Daughters of the Republic will never believe that I didn't do it to them on purpose. I was only in my early twenties, and I had no concept of what it took to line up a parade. I developed this plan which looked, on paper, something like a spiral. I would concentrate the parade entries in a spiral-like shape on the parking lot of the football field, and then I would unwind the spiral as the parade began its way along the boulevard towards downtown.

But when the parade stepped off, the spiral collapsed, and entries went helter-skelter down the boulevard, much to the chagrin of the announcer in the reviewing stand who had no idea what might be coming next. I waved and waved. I shouted and shouted. But there was no stopping the momentum once it began. The spiral failed completely. The middle of the spiral contained the horses, which everyone knows must come last in any parade. But the horses moved ahead of the far side of the spiral, which most unfortunately contained the Daughters of the Republic's float and the brigade of foot marching historical women. Unable to stop the disaster, I gave up and ran to hide, perhaps forever.

The Daughters of the Republic were left to march along down the street following the horses and breaking ranks when necessary.

I had no idea what would happen to me following this parade. No one had ever dared say one word of criticism against the Daughters of the Republic, much less position them side-stepping behind the horses in the parade. I assumed I was as good as fired from the newspaper.

However, when Ed came in *The Inquirer* on the following Monday morning, he asked me to go down to the Alcalde for coffee with him again. I was filled with apprehension as I followed him through the lobby and up to the screen door. These guys had almost fried me for running a small picture of a black bride in the newspaper. Imagine what they would do to me for making the Daughters of the Republic step in it.

When I slipped inside the coffee shop, my mouth rested on my chest. The entire group of men gave me a standing ovation as I followed Ed to a counter barstool. I think it was the proudest honor I have ever received.

THIRTEEN PIGS AND HAUTE CUISINE

The annual trauma for any country editor is, without doubt, the junior livestock show.

During that one week of the year, any vestiges of journalistic principles are suspended. Every small-town reporter scrambles to take pictures of scrawny kids with fluffed-up sheep as if newspaper time and space were infinite.

The editor realizes, of course, that he is not just taking a picture of little Bobby Smith and his white-ribboned, participation-prized steer with the hair-drier blown tail. He is shooting an almost metaphysical photograph of Smith family pride. The family from oldest to youngest has invested hope and effort into that steer, often sacrificed for it, and it is a matter of some standing for the Smith family with the agricultural community how high that animal places in the junior livestock show.

For all the Smith families, I have the empathy of someone who has survived the same disaster. My particular downfall was pigs.

The pig business is a teaching experience, and I could have appreciated the degree from the Pig College of Hard Knocks more if the tuition hadn't been so high.

I grew up on a now-defunct dairy farm, and I might have been a farmer . . . might have been, except that I had no aptitude. My grandfather had run enough Jersey cattle to supply the town with butterfat-rich milk, but as pasteurized and homogenized cartons came to town, the family dairy farm was down to milking only a dozen fawn-colored cows a day and delivering it to those few traditional souls who still believed milk should come in bottles. Father dropped off the milk on his way to his town job. Working in town was no problem as long as he had an eldest son, me, to whom the farm chores could be assigned.

But I was saved in the mid-1950s when the Soil Bank came along, and father discovered with open-mouthed jubilance that the government would pay him money for not planting crops or not milking cows. Clearly, he could make more money not farming than he could make farming, so we became devoted soil bankers and abandoned the dairy cows, save a couple we needed for our family supplies of milk. All I had to do was the maintenance of the land which the government required to keep our precious soil banker status.

Thus freed, I had time for walking down the Main Street sidewalks after school.

Something in small towns senses when a kid has time on his hands, and I found myself quickly approached by the man who owned the local newspaper. He needed a youth to sit atop a high stool and "catch" the newspaper sheets as they rolled off an old flatbed Babcock press. Otherwise, the sheets would sometimes sail onto the ink-grimed floor which made them unsuitable for folding and mailing to otherwise incredibly tolerant subscribers. The job paid 25 cents for a two-hour press run.

"Twenty-five cents for only two hours of sitting on a stool?" I could not believe it. I was rich, and I had found a vocation worthy of my leisurely inclinations — all at the same time. In those days, I could go to the town's picture show and see the latest Saturday afternoon western for nine cents, buy a piece of gum for a penny, and still have 15 cents left over for the following week. Just how good could life possibly be?

Father allowed that I could go into town every Thursday and work at the newspaper for a "cash money job." After all, he had a good stand of my siblings coming up to do the now-lessened farm work.

So I became a "newspaperman" to escape the dairy, and I began working my way up from press catcher to capture the highest position to which I was able to aspire: Printer's devil.

But the farm always seemed to reach out and grab me. One day, I announced to father that I was going into the pig business. An opportunity to buy a Hampshire boar and two gilts from the corn-fed pig country of Iowa had been too great to pass up, I explained. Not only would I make money raising pigs, but I would prosper by charging fees for the poor sows of the county to be bred to my pedigreed Iowa stud hog, which could also be my Future Farmers of America project for school.

In my high school which taught English as a foreign language, four years of FFA were mandatory, and my agriculture teacher loved it when a student had a project which earned the $500 necessary to become a "state farmer," an honor high enough to bring acclaim to the teacher as well. My pigs would do that for both of us.

Father cautioned me that the pig business was trickier than it looked, but it was my own money, so he gave me free rein.

For a few months, things went well. The boar won first place in the county livestock show, even with me showing him, which demonstrated that he was clearly a blue-ribbon animal. Trailers containing sows began to show up regularly to breed with this boar, and our gilts had farrowed five little Hampshires each making 13 pigs in all, a most unlucky number as it turned out.

But Iowa hogs grow huge. Before long, the boar was shoulder high, bigger than our cows. Even Father never went into his pen without an ax handle in hand. The thousand-pound monster boar collapsed any of the county's much smaller sows brought to breed with him. His massive body pushed their bellies to the ground with their four feet sticking out in all directions. We attempted building a breeding crate to support the boar's weight, but breeding in this fashion didn't seem to take, and soon the trailers and the cash breeding fees they represented stopped coming.

Meanwhile, the 13 ate and ate and ate. They were eating me into overdraft. The maize crop I planted specifically to feed the pigs failed completely, and not one little red grain of it could be salvaged for the voracious appetites. These pigs could eat a hundred-pound bag of grain from the feed store before I could get it poured into the trough. The feed store bill had grown so big that I calculated that I would have to sit on that stool and catch newspapers for more than two decades just to pay it. It was obvious that I would not only fail to earn $500 to become a state farmer, it appeared I might become the county's first Future Farmer of America to have to declare bankruptcy because of his school project.

I was desperate for pig food. I combed every road in the county for pickup loads of careless weeds, which pigs loved. I begged at the back doors of the town's cafes for any slop the cooks would give me. I climbed in the garbage bins behind the grocery stores to salvage any lettuce peelings which may have been discarded. I was shameless.

Anything I threw into the pen with those pigs was instantly devoured, and they were oinking for more before I could climb back into the pickup.

But as winter blew onto the prairie, my pig plight grew as bleak as the approaching sky of northers. Winter meant I had to feed the pigs without the help of pickup loads of careless weeds. Somehow, I had to keep these hogs alive until spring when they could be sent to market. Then I would know exactly how many years of paper catching would be required to pay back the money I had lost.

As I was finishing my work at the newspaper one cold evening in early December, a farmer named Willie Roy came by to see me.

"J. Tom," he said, "I've heard you need something to feed your pigs, right?"

"Do I. Oh, do I ever."

"Well," Willie Roy said thoughtfully, "I reckon I could let you onto my back field, that 30 acres the other side of the branch. I've got the full 30 acres planted in turnips. I've already harvested all I can sell, and the rest are just going to rot in the ground. You can pull up all you want for your pigs."

I thanked him and thanked him again. I felt like dropping to my knee and kissing the back of his hand. I could fill a high-sided trailer full of turnips and feed the pigs through the winter. I was saved.

Early Saturday morning, I cranked up the old Farmall 20 tractor and hooked the trailer onto the back of it. Ignoring an increasingly stiff north wind, I drove through the fields for a couple of miles until I had reached Willie Roy's land. The tractor dipped down through the branch and up the other side to the turnip field.

As I tossed turnips over the high sides and into the trailer, the wind began to bring freezing rain down upon me, but I labored away. I didn't want to miss the chance to gather a ton of pig food. All day long, I withstood the cold wind and rain to lob turnips into the trailer. When the sides of the trailer would hold no more, I tried to start the Farmall 20. I cranked and cranked until my arm was sore, but the weather had made the engine too cold and damp to fire up. Dark was settling in and the cold rain was turning to sleet, so I was finally forced to give up and walk home.

Early Sunday morning, I was attacking the turnip problem once again. After a day of rain, the north wind had brought a night of scattered sleet which had blown into piles along the fences and tree lines. Sunday was almost as miserable as Saturday, but I was determined to bring those turnips back to feed my ravenous hogs that very weekend.

I succeeded in building a fire underneath the Farmall 20, which warmed it up enough that my cranking caused it to sputter, cough, and then finally start. I climbed onto the tractor seat and began to pull the wagon of turnips back towards home. However, yesterday's rain had softened the branch to such an extent that the big wheels of the Farmall sank down in it like stepping off into a hog wallow. Try as I might, I could not free the tractor. For a couple of hours, I attempted to dig it out with a shovel, but the Farmall only bogged deeper into the mire.

As the wind picked up and I neared frostbite, I could think of no other solution except to walk to the nearest farmhouse and borrow a tractor of similar size to pull the Farmall out. This process took several chilling hours, but at last I pulled the Farmall and trailer onto solid land, returned the neighbor's tractor, walked back to the Farmall, cranked it up, and headed for home just as the December sun was making its early exit.

Two terrible days of labor and frustration had been invested in these turnips, and I was bone frozen, muddy wet, and exhausted. But as I drove towards the barnyard, a feeling of triumph began to build inside of me. Truly, I had gone through hell, but it would be worth it to have a winter's worth of pig feed. I even managed to sing a little through cold cracked lips.

Twilight colored the farmyard as I pulled the tractor and trailer up beside the barn. I leaped from the tractor seat onto the top of the trailer and scooped an armful of turnips into the pig pen.

"Come and get it," I yelled to the hogs as they grunted hungrily up to the fence. "You can feast forever."

The pigs ran over to the turnips, sniffed at them for a couple of seconds, then turned and walked away.

I could not believe my eyes. Nothing had ever hit the ground inside that pig pen that they didn't gobble up in seconds. Those pigs would even eat at my socks if I would stand still for it.

"Hold it, you silly pigs," I screamed, although I admit that "silly" may not have been the exact adjective I chose.

"Those are turnips. I worked hard for two freezing days to bring them to you. Now eat them."

The pigs ignored me and returned to the sheltered corner of their pen.

I was stunned. I leaped into the pen, picked out the littlest pig, and chased him down. I held him while I pried his mouth open and pounded a small turnip into his throat. The pig chewed and sputtered for a second or two; then he spit the entire turnip out onto the ground.

Before a rooster could crow the sundown, I was banging on the door of Willie Roy's farm house.

"Why didn't you tell me before I went to all that work," I asked him, "that pigs won't eat turnips?"

"Is that a fact?" Willie Roy said from behind his door. And then he added with such a flat country wit that it took me years to appreciate his humor: "Perhaps if you peeled the turnips, sliced them thinly, and marinaded them in a light sauce of butter and spices with a touch of parsley on the side . . . ."

Despite a wagon load of rotting turnips that the pigs never touched, I survived through the winter. Although he probably didn't have the money, Father paid the feed store until I could sell the pigs in the spring and cover most of my losses.

I learned not only to hold farmers in the highest regard but also to think a project through before undertaking it. Whenever I start something at the newspaper, I say to myself:

"Remember, pigs won't eat turnips."

THE STOMPING SAVIOR OF THE TENT REVIVAL

An editor in rural America knows he's in trouble when he peers out from among the stalagmite piles on his desk and sees a local church delegation coming to pray for him.

As they fill his newsroom and drop down on their knees to ask God to deliver this heathen newspaperman, the editor realizes that his flippant column has offended a central force in community life, and no possible penance will be too great a price to pay.

A morally correct minister, the only one of the flock allowed to remain standing when they collectively try to coax the Almighty into the devil's newspaper, clasps his preciously worn Bible to his breast and begs forgiveness for the unrepentant who are present, while the editor glances around the office in the futile hope someone else might be present and tries to recall which of his harmlessly humorous musings might have touched off this missionary effort.

Was it when he wrote that the notoriously long-winded town mayor would deliver the chamber of commerce banquet's invocatory prayer and "bore God"? No, everyone laughed over those words. Even the mayor had to admit it was funny.

Besides, these weren't the mayor's lay-peers. It is almost a requirement of political office in small southern towns that the mayor be a Baptist, or at the very least a Methodist. These kneelers, who were praying so intensely that many had tears running down their cheeks, had escaped from the The Bible Church over on the poor white side of town, a side the editor inherently understands from his own heritage.

When the word "Bible" appears in the name of a church, that usually signals a fundamentalist, independent, evangelical congregation who truly believe that it adheres literally to everything in the Good Book, even down to the imperfections in the printing. If the Bible is God's inspired word on earth, how could anything be wrong with it or with their interpretation of it?

Although I was naively new enough in the newspaper con actually to believe that readers might have occasional concerns about the truth, I had the seasoning to recognize that I had gotten myself into peril of eternal damnation with that little column item about the street preacher.

The Bible Church, as it turns out, was "in revival," and it had sponsored an old-fashioned Ozark tent revival preacher named Brother Bob to convert as much of the town as was salvable from the sins of the secular life. Brother Bob believed in taking Christ's message to the unbelievers, so he stood on the town square waving his Bible, screaming scripture at passing cars, and barking up business.

Little country towns don't have that many diversions, and the junior college history professor, Patrick, and I found it interesting to sit on the sidewalk curb outside the drugstore and listen to Brother Bob for a while.

Brother Bob was one of those ministers who were heavily accented with preacher whine and who pronounced the name "Jay-e-sus" in three syllables. I had been captivated by his major theological argument.

"The Bible," Brother Bob yelled to the driver of a bread delivery truck who was made captive audience by the town's only stop light, "says that it will remove our sins farther than the East is from the West.

"Farther than the East is from the West," he repeated

THE STOMPING SAVIOR OF THE TENT REVIVAL   31

as preachers who understand the simplicity of their audiences often do. "Do you know how far that is?"

The driver of the bread truck diverted his eyes back to the red light and drummed his fingers on the steering wheel. He clearly had no idea how far the East is from the West.

"Farther than the East is from the West," Brother Bob rang out in sing-song. "This demonstrates the Bible's great truth. Notice, mister, you there in the bread truck, just notice that the Bible doesn't say farther than the North is from the South. Hey, you in the bread truck, do you know why the Bible didn't say farther than the North is from the South?"

The driver of the bread truck wouldn't look back at Brother Bob. He was in hell and learning the meaning of eternity as he waited for the light to change.

"The Bible," Brother Bob screeched in a voice that carried for two blocks, "didn't say farther than the North is from the South because of one simple truth." Brother Bob turned back towards those of us on the drug-store curb as the bread truck driver saw green and made good his escape. "Do you people who are content to sit on the curb of life rather than join in God's great work know what that simple truth is?"

Patrick and I shook our heads, "No." And Patrick whispered to me: "This is going to be good."

"The truth," said Brother Bob waving his Bible, "is that the East is farther from the West than the North is from the South."

"Huh?" I heard Patrick say.

"Most people don't know," the preacher continued, "that the East is farther from the West than the North is from the South. But the Bible knows. Yes sir, the Bible knows this great truth. You ask me how the Bible knows the East is farther from the West than the North is from the South?"

"I didn't ask him," Patrick whispered again.

Brother Bob came a couple of steps threateningly closer to our curb: "Let me explain why the East is farther from the West than the North is from the South. If you fly an airplane from the North Pole toward the South Pole, it's a long flight, but pretty soon you reach the South Pole, and then you're going North again. After a few hours, you're back over the North Pole. The North and South Pole are far apart, but not as far as the East is from the West. If you begin flying West, you never stop. You just keep going West forever and ever, amen. You can go west for years or even centuries, and yet you never start going East. Therefore, the East is much farther from the West than the North is from the South."

Brother Bob pounded on his Bible with his smug conceit showing: "Praise the Lord for revealing this great truth."

Patrick and I bit our lips and tried to restrain ourselves from laughing aloud over Brother Bob's great revealed truth, but I enjoyed his little story so much that I repeated it in my newspaper column. I retold it faithfully without comment for even young editors understand not to make fun of anyone's religion. But unfortunately, I quoted Patrick as using one adjective to describe Brother Bob's little illustration: "Sophistry."

After Brother Bob looked sophistry up in the dictionary, he railed from his July hot tent pulpit against the Antichrist journalist and egghead friend Patrick who had attacked his ministry, and he anointed a lost tribe of disciples to trek down to the newspaper and pray me into submission.

It worked. Brother Bob's anguished band of soon prostrate prayer chanters had me in apology within minutes, and when several broke into the speaking of tongues and something resembling epilepsy on the newsroom carpet, I capitulated. What would they have Patrick and me do to make up for this one-word affront?

The devout Bible church mob would settle for only one thing: A chance to convert the two of us. So I agreed that

Patrick and I would attend that evening's revival service in the parking lot for trucks near the chicken-processing plant on the edge of town.

The big-top tent stood in faded colors and patchy tatters like something Ringling Brothers had discarded as Patrick and I parked along the shoulder of the highway. Our eyes first focused on popcorn, soft drink and hot dog stands just inside the gate.

"This is a circus," Patrick complained.

But remembering my promise to the prayer warriors, I tried to be more charitable: "Even the faithful have to eat, Patrick."

"All they are supposed to need is a fish and a couple loaves of bread to feed multitudes," Patrick said dourly. Journalists are supposed to be the cynics in the town, but I had learned through association with Patrick that reporters are wide-eyed children compared to the cynicism of history professors.

As we approached the entrance to the big top, a lesser funeral tent caught our eye. A line had formed out from under the canopy to this sideshow, and the people waiting explained that if Patrick and I wanted to be healed tonight, we must first be interviewed inside. Even though my allergies were acting up, we passed on being healed and went through a line of down-on-their-luck security guards into the main arena.

Although we had arrived half an hour early, we had to sit in the back since the big tent had already almost filled with a lower socioeconomic group which had come both to worship and be entertained, not necessarily in that order.

And Brother Bob could entertain. After two songs by the congregation and two from a hardened fallen angel, Brother Bob bounded onto the dais and breathed twenty minutes of hellfire and damnation, a caliber of which can only be learned by doing time in the Huntsville State Prison and Theological Seminary. Then after passing the collection buckets and threatening everyone to Hades if they didn't tithe, Brother Bob took off his sweat-stained jacket and began to minister to the frail and doomed.

The line to be healed filed into the big tent but still stretched out of sight back into the funeral tent. Like a mind reader, Brother Bob knew details about each person to be subjected to the laying on of hands. After a brief interview in which the preacher determined that medical science had failed to cure this person, Brother Bob placed one hand behind the person's neck and raised his other arm high above his head. Suddenly, the circling arm would descend downward and deliver a palm-first blow to the sick person's forehead with a war cry: "Be healed!"

I was unprepared for what happened when Brother Bob smote them. I had seen faith healers on television before, but the cameras never captured the shock of it all. When the blow from Brother Bob's palm smacked against the forehead, the body of the person being healed left the platform. Even men and women with seven or eight decades of life behind them leapt two feet upwards with arms and legs flailing the air behind their backs. They looked as if they had suddenly been grounded to a jolting current of electricity.

The shabby security guards rushed forward to catch the person being shocked with Holy Spirit when the electrifying Brother Bob let them go. Otherwise, the person being healed might have tumbled off the dais and onto the ground. Most were "slain in the spirit," which means the security guards placed them in irregular lines upon the hay spread to keep the ground dust down in front of the podium. Others seemed to receive a somewhat lessened shock, and with the aid of the guards, they could return to the slightly elevated platform to throw away their crutches or to declare with certainty that the liver cancer deep inside their bodies was now gone.

After he had healed a dozen terminal cases and the miraculous was beginning to become mundane, Brother Bob faced a voluptuous young woman, maybe 20 years of age, who came to be cured of her "bad temper." This was just the comic relief the Brother Bob show needed to keep the tent crowd on the edge of its seats. Brother Bob rolled up one sleeve and said that this healing was going to require an especially large dose of the Holy Ghost. He backed up to the far side of the stage and ran toward the ill-tempered siren to increase the velocity of his palm smack.

Brother Bob must have turned up the voltage on his Holy Spirit hand almost to electrocution level. When he touched the young woman, arms and legs went in all directions and her body waved like a wind-popped flag. She flew from the dais and into the arms of the scrubby catchers, who dragged her back towards the funeral tent with her toes making two little trenches in the topsoil.

Brother Bob laid hands on perhaps a half dozen more of the desperately ill, and then with the line of interviewed and suppposedly dying people still stretching out of sight into the side tent, he announced abruptly that this portion of the service was over. He casually told all of those awaiting his healing hand to come back tomorrow night.

"If they are still alive," Patrick whispered to me from his aisle seat in the back of the big top. "Can you believe he would heal only for 20 minutes and then stop with all those people still in line?"

"Perhaps the Holy Ghost is tired," I whispered back.

"Perhaps Brother Bob's battery is running out of juice," my cynical friend suggested.

But Brother Bob wiped his forehead with a towel, and with tears streaming down his face he addressed the crowd in an unknown Pentecostal tongue, a phrase of gibberish he repeated over and over. In seats ahead of ours, the tent congregation shouted back equally unintelligible chants which were each slightly different in syntax and sound from any other but somehow remarkably similar.

Once the tongues rang out all over the audience, Brother

Bob assumed his most serious posture and began his most important invitatory pitch to save souls, to convert lives, to raise money.

"Somewhere in this hot, sweaty tent is someone who has just heard the call of the Holy Spirit," Brother Bob yelled into his hand-held microphone. "God is tugging at the heart strings of someone here to make the biggest possible sacrifice. God is telling this person to follow Jay-e-sus. Yes, follow Jay-e-sus. Somebody say, Praise God!"

"Praise God!" voices of the audience answered.

Then he interrupted his prattle to confide: "You know, my friends, the Bible says the rich man asked Jay-e-sus what he could do to earn eternal life, Jay-e-sus told the rich man to sell everything he owned, give it to the poor, and follow Christ. And the man went away sad, for he was exceedingly wealthy. Somebody say, Praise Jay-e-sus!"

"Praise Jesus!" came the retort.

"God has just told me that His Son, Jay-e-sus, has just said the same thing to someone in our congregation here tonight. That unbeliever has felt the Holy Spirit come into his heart, but he is resisting. He is afraid to make the big commitment. Yes, brothers, he is afraid. Somebody say, "Praise God!"

"Praise God!"

"But when he asked Jay-e-sus what he must do, the Son of God told him as plainly as I am talking to you: Sell everything you own, give all your dirty old money to Brother Bob's Ministry, and follow me. Somebody say, Praise God!"

"Praise God!"

"My friend, you know who you are, Jay-e-sus is talking to you. He is telling you to give up the sins of the world. Yes, in the name of sweet Jay-e-sus, you must give up the sins of the world. Sell everything you own, and give it to God. Give it to Brother Bob's Ministry so that others can be saved. Somebody say, "Praise God!"

"Praise God!"

"So others can be saved. What profit a man if he gain the entire world and lose his immortal soul? Somebody say, 'Praise God!'"

"Praise God!" came the cry from the corners of the tent.

"Jay-e-sus is speaking to you, mister rich man. Don't lose your immortal soul. Follow Christ, and give all those sinful worldly things to Brother Bob's Ministry. You know who you are. Now I want you to stand up at your seat, walk right down this middle aisle, and commit your life to God and your wealth to his service. Jay-e-sus is pulling at your arm this very second. You can feel Him, so stand up and come down here to Christ."

Suddenly, and to my everlasting shock, I felt Patrick stand up beside me. When I looked, he was already walking down the middle aisle towards the dais with a focused eye and a determined stride. I had never seen the history teacher display such purpose.

Almost as surprised as I was, Brother Bob couldn't stop his mouth from falling open onto his microphone. Obviously, he always began his fishing for souls with an attempt to reel in the big one, the wealthy man or woman who endows his ministry with thousands, but after assessing this crowd, Brother Bob was just going through the routine until he could retreat to luring the hundred dollar givers, of which there could be quite a few. But a rich man willing to sell everything and follow Brother Bob's Ministry? His face turned to light. This was too good to be true.

"Welcome, welcome, brother," Bob said as he stretched his arms out wide to greet a Patrick marching single-mindedly down the center aisle, "into the embrace of God. Come let me save your immortal soul."

But Patrick continued on his course to the front row of seats where he raised his hand and swatted a huge stinging scorpion off the collar of a woman's dress. When the scorpion hit the hay-strewn ground, Patrick hopped and danced around until he could stomp on the scorpion repeatedly. When Patrick knew the scorpion no longer posed a threat, he looked up at a stricken Brother Bob and said:

"To hell with my immortal soul. I only wanted to save this woman's neck."

With that, Patrick turned and walked back up the aisle as a comatose Brother Bob allowed the microphone to fall down beside his thigh.

"Come on, let's go," Patrick said when he reached the back row, "I've had enough."

By this time, I had started to laugh uncontrollably, and departing seemed prudent. I could not glance back, but as best I could tell Brother Bob remained motionless and speechless until we had crawled under the side of the big top and out into the summer night.

I've laughed about that night with my history-teaching friend many times since then, and we've concluded that there are at least a couple of lessons to be gleaned from the scorpion-stomping incident.

Firstly, I have never again attached any negative term to anyone's religion in the newspaper. The lesson has been learned so well I can even treat New Age crap as if it made a cubit of sense. And I have been spared additional prayer sessions inside the newsroom.

And secondly, I have decided not to carry guilt about any embarrassment to Brother Bob's Ministry. After all, can you imagine the real two-syllable Jesus knocking off for the night with the line to be healed still reaching outside the tent?

THE NIGHT THE UFO LANDED IN THE FRONT YARD

A popular television show begins with the rather incredible claim:

"For every mystery, there is someone, somewhere who knows the truth."

In the great mystery of my youngest reporter days, that someone turned out to be Sheriff Homer T. Melton.

The whole thing began innocently enough in the living room of my family's little frame prairie house a couple of miles short of the Salt Fork of the Brazos River. I was a printer's devil at the *County Herald*, and I fancied myself a brilliant, if still budding, reporter. Clearly I was destined to line the wall with Pulitzer Prizes . . . if only I could get out of high school.

My mother and I were seated in the arm chairs squinting at the electronic snow of a television set straining to pick up a little programming from the nearest city big enough to have a television station, some 60 miles away. My sister and her boyfriend were sitting on the well-worn couch facing the front window. The younger kids were already in bed, and Papa was gone somewhere. That meant I was nominally the man of the house, a role I took seriously at age 17.

All of a sudden, the eyes of my sister and her boyfriend grew as big as country fried eggs. Simultaneously, they stood up in unison from the couch and stared out the front window with mouths agape.

"Something landed in our front yard!" my sister exclaimed. "It is brightly colored and glowing, and it came down right outside that window." The boyfriend agreed.

I performed an entrechat from my chair and quickly but cautiously moved to the window and peered out, but I could see nothing.

"Be careful, Bubba . . . something's out there. It had flashing lights. It has to be a flying saucer," my nearly hysterical sister cried. The boyfriend agreed.

I dashed to the kitchen closet and pulled out my ever-ready box camera and my trusty 20 gauge double-barreled shotgun as I stuffed shells and extra film into my pockets. I might have been a cub reporter, but I knew a Pulitzer in the making when I saw one. After all, it was common knowledge that Unidentified Flying Objects seemed to prefer the wide-open spaces of the great Southwest, and it was only logical that one might pick this sparsely populated prairie town as a place to put down. The reporter who got the first real picture of an extraterrestrial being puttering around in mother's sunflower garden would be famous forever.

As I rushed toward the front door, my mother grabbed my arm.

"Please don't go outside, J. Tom," she pleaded desperately. "We don't know what's out there."

"A good reporter always has to cover the news, Mom," I responded. "I intend to get a photograph of that flying saucer."

With my sister looking over my shoulder and the boyfriend safely standing behind her, I opened the front door just a crack and looked out into the yard. I could see nothing.

After a couple of seconds, I shook off my grasping, crying mother and stepped out into the front yard. It was a beautiful July evening full of sky and stars as only those prairie summers can be. Nothing seemed amiss.

THE NIGHT THE UFO LANDED IN THE FRONT YARD

When it was obvious that I wasn't being attacked by strange rays of light, my sister followed by the boyfriend came out behind me. Mother stood at the door and yelled for us to come back . . . or at least be careful.

"It must have landed out there on the county road," my sister concluded. The boyfriend agreed.

With camera held to my face and shotgun under arm, I sneaked down the lane to the county road to see this alien spacecraft which touched down so near to our house. A safe distance behind me, my sister and the boyfriend trailed along.

If a flying saucer had landed, it did so without making even one smooth spot in the relatively unmaintained county road. The pickup tire ruts were as deep as ever. The crickets chirped. The frogs croaked. The prairie was undisturbed.

"It must have come down farther away than it looked," my sister allowed. "I'll bet it landed just beyond the sand hill over in Sam Ferguson's field." The boyfriend agreed.

So we climbed in the family pickup, and ignoring the protests from mother, we drove to the other side of the sand hill. Nothing.

"I know it landed just over there," my sister said. "I think it was so big that it looked really close. But I am positive that it landed no farther away than the Stubbs' mesquite pasture." The boyfriend agreed.

We made ever-widening circles as we searched for this brilliant and fearsome object my sister kept insisting came to earth near us. Her boyfriend continued to agree. The Stubbs' pasture was as serenely moonlit as a picture postcard, and so were the adjoining fields. The shotgun was unloaded
and placed underneath the pickup's seat.

After half an hour of fruitless searching, we decided to drive into town to see if the National Guard had yet been summoned to quell the statewide panic. To our surprise, the three straight blocks which the natives called "downtown" with no hint of a smile were typically bereft of activity. A couple of cars sat at the Dairy Queen with no hint of urgency.

At the end of the High Noon street stood Sheriff Melton, the law east of Buzzard Peak, leaning against his county vehicle. He was carrying on an occasional conversation with the town's night watchman.

By this time, I had begun to suspect that the light that "landed in our front yard" might not prove to be the worldwide flash story I had anticipated. I approached the sheriff a bit gingerly.

"Has anybody reported seeing anything unusual tonight?" I asked him.

A true frontier lawman, he took a long time before he responded. There was no hurry. "Unusual?"

Obviously, he was going to make me commit first.

"I mean, unusual like something in the sky," I said.

Again, there was the long lawman pause. Then the sheriff said dryly: "Oh, you must be talking about the meteor which flashed across the sky about an hour ago. Spectacular thing that. People saw it all over Texas, Oklahoma, and New Mexico. They say it burned up over Arizona. Why do you ask?"

"Oh, no reason," I answered in my best attempt to muster aplomb. "We just saw it and wondered. We were pretty sure it was only a meteor."

Then we drove back home.

"We looked like a bunch of dopes," I said to my sister. The boyfriend agreed.

HORSEFEATHERS AND THE VIRGIN MARY

Small towns seem to have more than their pro rata of characters, and almost all of them make the newspaper their second home.

Obviously, big cities have characters too, but I doubt that metropolitan residents can get to know their oddballs as we can in rural areas. And what good is a town's weirdo if you don't get to enjoy him every few days over a cup of coffee? Huge daily newspapers have fortress lobbies with security guards to keep out the characters. In small town newspapers, the nuts walk right in with the regular folks.

When I first came to town, I heard about this fellow called Horsefeathers, who maybe ran or maybe even owned the Eastside Ice House bar on the east side of the railroad tracks. By all accounts, Horsefeathers had a schizophrenic personality which could be alternately brilliant or unable to focus on making twenty cents in change.

During one of his lucid moments, he came prancing into the newspaper in a rhinestone cowboy shirt, carrying a wallet-sized color photograph of a small girl.

"Hello, I'm Horsefeathers. Expect you've heard of me."

I allowed that I had heard his rather unforgettable name.

"This," he said holding up the photo with nicotined fingers, "is my granddaughter from Arizona. I want you to run her picture in the paper."

"Well . . . uh," I stammered as I took the snapshot from him, "we usually need some kind of news angle to run someone's picture in the newspaper. Has she won any awards or anything? She's a cute little girl, but why should we run the photograph of a child who lives so far away?"

"Because," he responded with flashing eyes, "she is Horsefeathers's granddaughter."

"Well . . . uh," I continued to stutter as I shifted the papers on my desk to buy excuse time. "Uh . . . we, uh . . . we normally need some kind of reason before we can run a picture in the newspaper."

"You need a reason to run her picture?" Horsefeathers puffed up with indignation. "I'll give you a reason. If you don't run her picture in the newspaper, I will ride my horse into this newspaper office."

"You will what?"

"I will ride my horse into the newspaper office," he stated flatly. "Just ask anyone in town if I won't. Just ask over at First National Bank. I rode my horse right into the bank lobby and made a deposit on the floor."

I laughed because I had previously heard several references to this historic town event.

"And," Horsefeathers continued, "I will make a deposit on the newspaper floor as well. Is that reason enough?" He pushed back his hat with the colored hawk feather in it.

"Yes," I admitted, "that sounds like as good a reason as I ever heard to run a picture in the newspaper. It will be in next week's edition."

The photograph ran on page 7 with the explanation that the child was the granddaughter of Horsefeathers. For the sake of journalistic honesty, I added in the cutline that Horsefeathers had threatened to ride his horse into the newspaper if the picture didn't appear, and everyone in town understood.

From that day, Horsefeathers and I felt like friends, and he frequently insisted I come over to the seedy Eastside Ice House where he drank more beer than he sold and where he trumpeted over his odd concerns of the day like a heldentenor. After a couple of beers, the most peculiar things would bother Horsefeathers. Never mind that unemployment in the nation had climbed above 8 percent. He had no intention of doing any serious work even if it dropped to a negative. Never mind if there was combat in Southeast Asia. Horsefeathers had lost his concern for war after being drafted during the Korean conflict and spending six weeks in the Army before his psychological discharge. Never mind if the president had just launched a war on poverty. Horsefeathers would say: "We're too poor to be in the poverty program. To be in the poverty program, you have to pay minimum wages, and these chicken farmers will never do that. I need to write the president and tell him that this county is just too poor to be in his war on poverty."

But late one hot summer afternoon while watching the local news which spewed out of the big city all too close to our town, Horsefeathers became enraged over a broadcast by Marvin Hudspeth, Eyewitness News. This "investigative reporter" with an eye for the sensational had "uncovered" an Indian burial ground in the adjoining county. Horsefeathers knew the report was a lie, he informed those of us in his ice house, because as a young man he had helped in the construction of that small cemetery site. Those were just regular old farm family bones, he assured us, and not some lost ancient tribe as insisted by Marvin Hudspeth, Eyewitness News.

"Marvin Hudspeth, Eyewitness News, will report anything, true or not," Horsefeathers contended with three-beer volume, "as long as it makes good television. If someone told him the Virgin Mary was appearing on the screen door of this beer joint, he would be up here to film it."

"I don't know, Horsefeathers," I softly responded in weak defense of my chosen field. "Journalists have a responsibility to check their facts. Marvin Hudspeth, Eyeitness News, might sensationalize a bit for the sake of ratings, but I doubt he would fall for something as lame as the Virgin Mary on a fly screen."

"Of course he would," Horsefeathers insisted, "and I will prove it."

As a matter of principle, I would never knowingly be a part of an outright journalistic hoax. In my tenure as a country editor, I have been the victim of a couple of bogus stories and the intended victim of dozens more which I managed to discover before going to print. But it never really occurred to me that a character like Horsefeathers could fool the state's biggest television station with such an idiotic idea.

And yet, a phone call came into the newspaper the following day. A very important sounding voice announced: "This is Marvin Hudspeth, Eyewitness News. What do you know about that image of the Virgin Mary on the screen door at the Eastside Ice House?"

As if a bucket of cold water had been thrown into my face, I felt nothing but shock. I didn't want to lie to this alleged television reporter, but my friendship for Horsefeathers restrained me from overtelling the truth.

"I've heard about it," I said, coming precariously close to periling my immortal soul.

That was all Marvin Hudspeth, Eyewitness News, needed to know. The television star said he would be at the newspaper office first thing in the morning and hung up the telephone.

"Oh boy," I said to myself as I slapped my palm against my forehead. "There is no telling what lies Horsefeathers has told that television station." I rushed over to Eastside Ice House where I found the cowboy of great leisure on his usual stool at the edge of the bar.

"Horsefeathers!" I demanded. "What did you say to Marvin Hudspeth, Eyewitness News?"

Instead of answering me, Horsefeathers took a long draw on his long-neck beer bottle. Then he said: "I didn't tell him nothin. Hell, he might be suspicious of me. I had Ruby tell him."

"What did you have Ruby tell him?"

Horsefeathers gave his beer bottle a circular shake as if to determine how much remained in the bottom before engaging in the kind of serious conversation certain to allow beer to grow warm.

"I had Ruby tell him that we got an image of the Virgin Mary on this here screen door."

"But Horsefeathers," I protested, "you lied to the television station."

"No," he said, "we got an image of the Virgin Mary right there on the screen." He pointed towards the front, and I turned to follow his finger. Sure enough, as the outside light shone behind the tiny squares of wire, an outline of a woman's face could be seen in lighter tones.

Horsefeathers put down his beer and walked over to the door. "Ain't it nice? You should see it when the morning light is streaming through."

"How did that get there?"

"It just appeared . . .," Horsefeathers said.

"Appeared, my foot."

"Appeared . . ., after I mixed a little dab of whitewash into a pint of paint remover and brushed it on."

"Horsefeathers, that's fraud. You can't let Marvin Hudspeth, Eyewitness News, broadcast something like this."

"Don't worry, Mister Editor," Horsefeathers smiled, "I'll get him straightened out before he takes to the air."

As I returned to the newspaper, I consoled myself that even Marvin Hudspeth, Eyewitness News, could not fall for something as transparent as that. Three minutes after he meets Horsefeathers, he will smell a pseudo-western rat, pack up his camera crew, and depart furiously on the drive back to the city.

"First thing in the morning" is not the same thing to

city people as it is to country folk. We think of "first thing" as being something about 8 o'clock, if not earlier. "First thing" was about 11 o'clock in the morning for this big city television crew, but just when I allowed myself to feel relieved that Marvin Hudspeth, Eyewitness News, had bothered to double check even one fact and realized the truth, the personality himself came bursting in the newspaper's front door.

"This is the way I see this story" were the first words out of his mouth as he approached me with his palms framing my desk. "This quaint little town is transformed by the miracle which has happened at Eastside Ice House."

I thought to myself: This is how he sees the story? He already has his angle, and he hasn't gathered one single fact to determine if it might be remotely true. Let the fool be fooled.

But Marvin Hudspeth, Eyewitness News, needed no input from me. He was talking at top forty disc jockey speed: "Now, I understand that this ice house is kind of the local dive, and since the image of the Blessed Virgin has appeared on its door, all the patrons have reformed, given up the Devil's alcohol, and are turning the beer joint into a quaint little shrine. Pilgrims are coming from everywhere to touch the Virgin and be healed by her amazing powers. We think this can go national."

What a line of bull Horsefeathers has shoveled upon this mental midget, I thought silently. Should I enlighten him? But any temptation to let Marvin Hudspeth, Eyewitness News, off Horsefeather's hook was dismissed as I heard his first demand:

"Now, give me a copy of what you have written about this so far . . . just for reference."

Like every television reporter I have ever known, he wanted me to hand him a newspaper with all the facts already checked out and written down so he could do "his own story" from them. Once at a big breaking news event,

I caught a big city television reporter who had ripped my story out of my typewriter and was standing in front of his cameras reading it as if it were his own. So I shaded the truth for Marvin Hudspeth, Eyewitness News:
"Actually, this is all too new," I said. "We haven't written anything about it yet."
"Oh," he didn't even bother to disguise his disappointment. "Then, take me out to the Eastside Ice House and let me meet this Ruby woman. What do you know about her?"
"Not much," I said, angered that he assumed I would drop whatever I was doing and escort his television crew around town. I didn't tell him that Ruby was the girl friend, or perhaps common law wife, of a character named Horsefeathers, but I did show him the way across the tracks to Eastside Ice House.

When we turned the last corner and could see the ice house, I gasped at a piece of staged theater which would have made Cecil B. DeMille proud. Horsefeathers had 50 people gathered outside the beer joint as if they were waiting to get in. Some even looked as if they had camped there overnight. We parked, and Marvin Hudspeth, Eyewitness News, tore through the crowd like a young boy heading for a carnival. His camera crew filmed every twitch of his eyebrows.

Inside the ice house, Horsefeathers had put up crosses and candles underneath the Miller's Beer neon sign and had pushed the broken-down tables back to permit a dozen weeping women to kneel on the floor and pray towards the front screen door where the late morning light streamed through the image of the Virgin Mary. But there was no sign of Horsefeathers.

Marvin Hudspeth, Eyewitness News, had found yellow-journalism heaven. He filmed the Blessed Virgin's face from every direction. He interviewed the worshipers about the miracle healing which had been occuring daily.

He was so enamored with the story that he even stepped off-camera long enough to let Ruby tell how she had discovered the blessed image by having to serve beer day and night on her poor arthritic ankle until two mornings ago when she stepped into the light of the screen door and felt her foot instantly cured. When she looked to see the source of the miraculous light, she saw the screen door and explained, "Mary, Mother of Jesus!"

Horsefeathers, I thought to myself.

But Marvin Hudspeth, Eyewitness News, bought it all. He filmed and filmed and filmed. Then it was time for him to do his all-important on-camera wrap-up before rushing back to the city in time to make the six o'clock news. He assumed his microphoned position beside the screen door:

"We all know God works in mysterious ways, and that is what is happening in this quaint little town where the Blessed Virgin Mary has transformed a den of iniquity into a holy shrine of prayer and healing."

And then he paused and cocked his head for his trademark emphasis: "This is Marvin, Hudspeth, Eyewit . . . ."

But before he could close out his wrap-up, Marvin Hudspeth, Eyewitness News, found himself sprayed with water coming through the screen door. As he gasped, Horsefeathers walked in the door with garden hose in hand. Horsefeathers sprayed the screen with thumb-pinched volumes of water from every angle.

A soaked Marvin Hudspeth, Eyewitness News, protested: "Wait, wait, stop! Aren't you washing off the image of the Virgin Mary?"

"Virgin Mary?" Horsefeathers laughed as he continued to squirt the screen door. "Naw, that's only . . . fly specks."

COWS HAVE NO RESPECT
FOR SCIENCE

John McAdams was a small-time dirt farmer tucked back into the piney woods when his 15 minutes in the spotlight fell upon him.

Actually, McAdams didn't come by fame accidentally but as the result of a newspaper promotion.

My little newspaper had added another publication day and needed some kind of promotion to make people notice our additional issue. So the newspaper staff dreamed up a plan which was almost as successful as William Randolph Hearst's igniting of the Spanish-American War to build circulation.

I was raised in the arid southwest where entire towns flourished or floundered by the sparse rainfall, and I had come to appreciate how much interest people have in whether they will be rained upon or not. And I had learned how difficult it is to forecast whether rain will fall in any one given spot.

The newspaper's plan was a simple one: We would find an old farmer who truly believed the folk methods of predicting the weather were more reliable than the scientific ones employed by the National Weather Service, and we would have a forecasting contest.

We had little trouble finding such a farmer. He was the very quiet-spoken John McAdams, who would swear in church that his cow, which he called Brahma, was a complete and accurate gauge of what the weather was going to do. McAdams never listened to the weather on the radio since it was always wrong. Instead, he watched how his Brahma acted every morning, and he knew without fail if a norther was blowing in or if rain would come down the following day.

McAdams was not the kind of guy who was easy to interview. Two words from him made a long sentence, and four words were an absolute dissertation. He had lived with his animals and worked a small plot of land on the edge of the forest all his life, and he was clearly more comfortable with critters than with folks. He spoke slowly in subdued tones and was too shy to look even home town people in the eye. While he talked, he plowed lines in the ground with the toe of his boot.

But despite the difficulties, we managed to do a story about McAdams' sincerely held belief that his cow, Brahma, could forecast the weather far better than the National Weather Service's prediction on television.

We ran the McAdams story on the front page of the newspaper, complete with his claim for Brahma, and soon we had a broadsheet page of letters supporting him or doubting him.

After a letters-to-the-editor debate in a couple of issues, the newspaper ran a story in which McAdams challenged the National Weather Service to a forecasting contest. We announced that a two-month-long forecasting contest would begin the following week.

I called the regional director for the National Weather Service and told him we wanted his latest and most accurate forecast for our county. He laughed the whole thing off and refused to add any scientific personality to what his office was already doing.

So the contest began. The lines were drawn on the very first day when the National Weather Service predicted no chance for any precipitation and a high of 80 degrees. McAdams forecast 72 degrees because Brahma wouldn't come out of the barn, which meant rain.

It rained two inches, and the high was only 71 degrees. The cow leaped into the lead.

The contest caught our readers' fancy almost immediately, and new subscriptions began piling up on the circulation desk . . . just as we had hoped.

But something else happened that we hadn't anticipated. The contest became an international event. It began with a feature story about the contest in the big city papers which the wire services carried all over the world.

As it turns out, the most important moments on local television come during the nightly news, and the weather is the dullest but most necessary portion of the most important part. Television stations were desperate to enliven their weather segments. When the city television stations learned about the contest between the cow and the forces of science, they descended upon our newspaper in droves and tried to make the contest their own.

Each night during the prime-time news, the television weathermen gave the National Weather Service forecast. Then they had a segment on how McAdams' cow, Brahma, acted and what McAdams said those actions meant. They gave the results of the contest to date, which had McAdams quickly building a substantial lead. Sometimes they could even capture McAdams on camera saying a few words in a row.

Soon, the national wire services had picked up the contest on a daily basis, and the newspaper was deluged with phone calls and visitors. The phone rang, and it was CBS News wanting to set an interview time. The phone rang again, and it was *Time* magazine coming for a story.

We worried about how the reclusive McAdams might hold up under all this attention. But we wasted a worry.

The timid farmer had come out of his cocoon and had emerged as a fully developed media butterfly. He talked so much into the microphone that even the chatty radio personalities could not force in their witticisms. He quickly became an expert on the best television camera angles for

Brahma as she ate from the trough beneath the lean-to shed attached to the weather-worn old barn.

Instant is not a fast-enough word for the kind of celebrity McAdams had become. He was on the television network morning shows. He was doing radio interviews daily with stations in Washington, New York, London, and Berlin. And he was winning the contest.

While McAdams was doing brilliantly, our little newspaper strained at the pressure. After all, we still had a newspaper to put out, and life in the community went on despite the weather forecasting contest. We were growing by scores of new subscribers daily, and we were on the telephone constantly to Australian television or some Italian magazine.

About three weeks into the contest, I picked up the phone to find a very angry head of the National Weather Service in Washington, D.C., on the other end. I had been expecting his call.

"Mr. Graham," he said bluntly, "the National Weather Service does not wish to participate in your so-called contest. We want it stopped. We will no longer cooperate."

"You're not cooperating already," I told him. "The only way you can stop participating is if you make no forecast for our county."

There was a moment of silence; then the agency head said: "I cannot do that. I am required by law to forecast for your county."

"Then you're in the contest. Good luck," I said.

Suddenly, he turned human: "You don't understand. Every morning that cow man is on the radio station here in Washington telling how Brahma can forecast better than our government agency. It is embarrassing. It is humiliating. He is making the National Weather Service the laughing stock of all D.C."

"Then I suggest you make the best forecast you can for our county and win the competition," I said.

"But it's not fair," he protested. "What is to keep

McAdams from watching the weather on television and picking up our scientific forecast as his own?"

"What's to keep your scientists from watching the cows and the other natural signs that McAdams uses?" I argued back. "This is a no-holds-barred contest. Your forecasting team can come out and watch Brahma in her barn if it wants to, and McAdams can listen to your forecasts if he likes. But whoever makes the most accurate forecast, using whatever method, is the winner."

The agency head snorted into the telephone a couple of times and hung up. However, he responded by sending a crack team and a truck load of the newest equipment to our previously ignored town. The official National Weather Service forecast for this county was no longer going to be a routine matter. It would be the best that 20th Century science could muster against the talents of that one old cow.

While McAdams' celebrity grew, his weather forecasting suffered, and slowly, the National Weather Service began to whittle down his once large lead.

But McAdams could no longer be bothered with attention to the contest. He had become an internationally known star. He would grab the microphone and begin talking at length while instructing the video cameraman how to get the light just right.

When NBC flew McAdams to Burbank to be a guest on Johnny Carson's Tonight Show, he was the funniest thing I ever saw, even if he was furious because NBC wouldn't foot the bill to fly out Brahma too.

Suddenly, he was getting paid for all of this. He was negotiating with several almanac companies for a regular feature in their annual books, and he was considering an agent to field the broadcast offers.

One morning as the contest neared its final week, McAdams balked at giving us his forecast unless our little newspaper came up with cash. He thought $5000 might be about right, considering all he had done for us.

The newspaper's circulation had gone up almost 2000

copies during this contest, but we were a small community paper which was not in a position to bid for the services of a celebrity against the likes of national magazines or syndicated television shows. We had created a monster. Finally, we persuaded him to complete the contest for a few fringe benefits . . . but no cash.

As the final forecast of the competition approached, McAdams' lead had been cut to one point. The winner hinged on the weather of that last day. McAdams said Brahma stayed in her shed, which in cow-speak indicated rain. The National Weather Service's instruments foresaw no chance of rain.

Fortunately, as it turned out, the day was beautiful with nary a drop of rain in the entire county. Science had prevailed by the narrowest of margins, but it had prevailed nonetheless.

And McAdams went back to his quiet but satisfying life as a piney woods farmer.

THE FEEL OF HAIR-FACE STUBBLE ON SPAIN'S HOTTEST HAND

Small-town American journalists should never be issued passports for more than two weeks at a time.

That kept going through my mind one cold winter's night while I stood beside a deserted highway in the middle of the Spanish plain. I was hitchhiking with nary a vehicle's headlight in sight for tens of kilometers and no prospect of reaching Zaragoza.

And to make things much worse, I had a traveling companion: A complaining young American woman who kept informing me that she would no doubt freeze to death before dawn. I had gotten her into this mess, she repeatedly and correctly reminded me, and I had better get her out of it.

Just how had I come to be abandoned late at night to the blowing north wind on the empty countryside of Spain? My cultural background deserved much of the blame. Those of us who grew up in the supportive rural communities of America came to think we could do anything, and my personality was cast in concrete before I discovered this might not always be the case.

My generation can perhaps remember when the thing to be was what we called a hippie, which was, I suppose, someone who everyone knew was "hip." A hippie supposedly traveled the country, or better yet the world, with fewer cares than the lilies of the field. He, or she, lived off the fat of the land, loved all living things and had sex with most of them, and cared naught for the material. A true hippie survived two notches below vagrancy and could successfully mooch off a bag lady. A true hippie had no home but was never homeless since he always crashed in someone else's pad. As it turned out, most true hippies had rich families.

More than anything, I wanted to be a hippie, but I could never quite pull it off. First of all, I knew better than to ask my kid-rich but resource-poor family for hippie money. This was the father who had taken his eldest boy aside and said to me: "Son, we want you to go to college . . . good luck." And in the second place, the farming community in which I was raised instilled the values of labor and self-reliance. Cotton farmers thought nothing of showing up at 5 a.m. to roust sleeping boys for two hours of changing irrigation pipes before school. A youth who earned the reputation of being a lazy worker had approximately the same standing in the town as a boy reputed to be a coward.

With this inherited handicap, I had no chance at true hippiedom. I could not force myself to ask for something I could earn on my own. I could never bring myself to waste the day. I didn't even know how to "groove."

But I could travel like a hippie, and isn't it almost incumbent upon every young journalist to learn something of the world? So when I completed university studies and had passed my draft board physical, I sold the trailer house bought while working my way through college, and I would use this $600 to explore Europe. I informed my hometown draft board how to get in touch with me through my father and American Express. (Regardless of what my generation thought of the Vietnam War, I could not be the first of my family and community to refuse to go when his country called.) I would return home when the official draft notice arrived or when the money ran out — whichever came first.

Very hippie-like, I slung my knapsack over my back, walked out onto the highway in front of the family farm, stuck out my thumb, and headed for Europe. Today, we think of hitchhiking as a dangerous gamble which should never be risked, but in the 1960's, hitchhikers were common as highway litter. I had already thumbed my way across the U.S. and back twice, and I loved the free feel of the open road with only my rucksack to slow me down. I considered myself a hitchhiking expert and would have written a book on the etiquette of this mode of travel had not the nasty turn of society destroyed the sport.

Hitchhiking in Europe proved even easier than in the States, and after six months I had been all over the continent without unpleasant incident of any kind. My only problem had been the American hippies who attached themselves to me at youth hostels since I appeared to have some small means of sustenance. I once had a hippie follow me all over Paris because he noticed I had the cash to buy a bag of pommes frites. I decided the American hippies were doing more damage to European relations in a day than the U.S. State Department could repair in a decade. Hippies even made Mark Twain's "Innocents Abroad" appear innocent. So I stayed away from the youth hostels entirely.

One of the basic tenets of hitchhikers is that having a female along increases the odds exponentially that any one given vehicle will stop and offer a ride. This was particularly true in Europe 30 years ago. Those continental men had read about the hippies and their "free love" attitudes, and who knew what might evolve if a hippie-ette could be enticed into an automobile? However, the hippie-ettes talked much more free love than they participated in, and most were exceedingly anxious to have the protection of a male companion along the roadsides, if nowhere else. Thus, I traveled to Spain in a symbiotic relationship with a Midwestern Puritan disguised in the sack dress garb of the day as an American hippie-ette.

We hitchhiked across the Pyrenees, thumbed our way to Madrid, down to Cordoba and Sevilla, then on to Gibraltar and into Tangier and North Africa. It had been our plan to come back through Portugal on the return trip, but virtually everyone kept asking if we were on our way to the St. Joseph's Day Festival in Valencia. Locals and traveling tourists alike raved about this annual event, and we decided that taking in a Spanish fiesta along the Costa Blanca would be more fun than Lisbon.

The decision proved a delightfully good one. Valencia during the week-long St. Joe's celebration is a sensual potpourri of morning tropical foods, afternoon bull fights, night street dances, and continuous parades of endless virgins, all of which combines for as much fun as mortals can tolerate. And because the festival falls during the European version of spring break, Valencia was overflowing with college students from all over the continent, which is why everyone assumed we were heading there.

On the exhausted Sunday morning following the climactic Saturday night, my female companion and I decided to depart wearily for Barcelona. Expert hitchhiker that I was, I knew precisely how to find the city bus which ran to the far north of Valencia where the Barcelona highway began. When we reached the highway, I poked my head forward at an unexpected sight. College students by the hundreds sought rides northward and lined every available foot of the road's shoulder. They even stood in line to belly up to the edge of the highway. In all my hitchhiking years, I had never seen a crowd one-one hundredth that big.

"We will require days to get out of Valencia," I complained to my companion. After we watched this scene for a couple of hours without being able even to get in position to wave for a ride, I made a decision to violate the major tenet of hitchhiking: Always keep to the main roads. I pulled out my map of Spain and suggested we take a much smaller road which departed Valencia to the northwest and snaked its way through the mountains toward Zaragoza. "I'll bet there'll be no hitchhikers on that road," I predicted.

We took the bus back into the center of Valencia and

another one out to the Zaragoza highway, and sure enough, the road had no hitchhikers. But it also had no cars.

"This is bad," I said to my companion. "There is so little traffic that we could get stuck halfway between Valencia and Zaragoza. It is essential we be certain that the car is going all the way to Zaragoza before we accept the ride."

While my analysis of our situation was flawless, my Spanish was not. When after several hours only a dozen vehicles had whizzed by, one car finally stopped. In my best schoolboy foreign language, I asked the driver if he va a la Zaragoza.

"Si," he answered.

To be certain, I pointed to the map and emphasized that the trip must wind up in Zaragoza by este noche. The answer was "si" once again, so we climbed into the backseat as a cold north wind began to blow.

For a couple of hours, we drove along the empty road toward Zaragoza, and just as the sun was escaping under the western horizon, the driver of the automobile stopped the car and told us to get out. He was, it seems, turning down an almost invisible road to the southwest, and he knew we wanted to continue northward to Zaragoza. I was stunned, but there was nothing to do but climb out onto the wind-blown Spanish plain.

"I thought you said he was going all the way to Zaragoza," my companion complained. "I thought you spoke some Spanish. Is your Spanish that bad?"

"I swear that's what he said," I answered. "We'll just have to catch another ride tonight."

"The last time I checked," she said sarcastically, "it was somewhat difficult to thumb a ride when there aren't any cars."

I looked back down the road we had just traveled. Since we were atop a gradual rise, we could view a dozen miles through the twilight: Nothing.

"How far is it to the next village," she asked.

"I estimate about 30 kilometers."
"How far is that in English?"
"About 19 miles. We can walk."
"We cannot walk," my companion said. "My feet hurt, and I am cold." Despite all the talk about being one with nature and living off the land, most hippies had no intension of being inconvenienced.

The temperature began to plummet after the sun disappeared. On this high plain, it was obvious the mercury would be near freezing before morning, and it would feel even colder in such a cutting north wind. I quickly constructed the best semi-shelter I could under the crest of the rise, and we stared out at the growing blackness in search of a headlight.

A couple of hours passed before we saw one in the distance. We had several minutes to assume our best friendly hitchhiker posture by the side of the road, female in front. But to our dismay, the car roared past us without even a hint of slowing down.

As two more hours passed, my companion began to shiver. "I am going to die," she said. "I will freeze to death on this hill. Put my grave right over there."

"You won't freeze," I said. "Another car will come by, and I promise I will not let this one go past us. I'll fall prostrate across the road and be run over first."

Forever later after a chilled 11 o'clock, another set of headlights finally appeared on the horizon. I leaped up and positioned myself in the middle of the highway where the vehicle could not pass. These headlights took forever to climb the long incline, and when they came close, I could see why. It was a rickety old flatbed truck stacked meters high above the tiny cab with crates of oranges. It could go no faster than 15 miles per hour up this hill, so it was almost stopped already as it approached. The groan of the engine eased as the truck pulled up beside me. Down rolled the window, and I looked into the miniature cab which was fully occupied by two very large Spanish men who looked like they had been on the road for three or four unshaven days.

Yes, they were going to Zaragoza. Yes, we could ride with them. But ride where? There was no room on the flatbed which had orange crates tied on so high they were making the vehicle lean. Before I could ask, the man sitting on the passenger side stepped out of the truck and indicated we should climb into the miniscule cab, which already contained two suitcases and a pile of at least 20 packages in addition to the two large Spanish workers.

'We are saved,'' I said to my female companion. "These two Spanish gentlemen will take us to Zaragoza."

"Where will we ride?" my hippie-ette friend inquired.

"We will somehow squeeze all four of us and our knapsacks into the truck cab," I said.

And after some effort, we succeeded in forcing all four people and assorted bags inside and closing the truck cab door. I was half-sitting, half-reclining on the back of the driver's seat with two knapsacks and a number of packages in my lap. My female companion was perched equally uncomfortably atop the back of the seat on the passenger's side with a suitcase and several packages covering her.

I began to thaw out as the truck shook its way along the road at a breath-taking 20 miles per hour. At this speed, all night would be required to reach Zaragoza, but I felt relieved and happy. It was warm inside. With the cab piled so high with bags and packages, I could not see the passenger side, so I made what light conversation I could with the cheerful driver.

Before the truck had gone five or six slow miles, my female companion announced: "I've got to get out of here."

"Are you kidding?" I could not believe what I had heard her say through the debris. "Have you forgotten that we were freezing out there? What could possibly make you want back out in that wind."

"This creep is putting his hands all over me," she reported.

I shifted around and moved knapsacks and packages

until I could see the grizzly farm worker sitting on the seat below her. I shook my finger at him: "No! No! No molesta la mujer."

He smiled up at me through his hairy face: "Si, si."

I leaned back against the top of the cab again. It had all been a misunderstanding. This kind and simple Spanish farm worker had watched Woodstock on television with all those wild American hippie women who believed in free love, and he had quite obviously made the idiotic assumption that some small portion of it might be true.

"He's doing it again," my companion reported amid the interior rubble. "I can't stand it. I've got to get out of this truck."

"Get out?" I could not imagine the idea. "So suffer a little. We must be only about ten miles from that little village I saw on the map. If we can just make it there, we can find a place to spend the night."

"How long will that take?"

"At this speed, I estimate about half an hour."

"I can't take it," she said. "He's all over me. I've got to get out."

The one thing we could not do, I said to myself, was leave this truck before we reach that village. I must find another solution. "Let me see what I can do to stop him," I said aloud, and I shifted forward once again through the packages until I could reach my arm around my companion's waist and ran my hand through the mishmash of bags and along her now exposed leg until, sure enough, I felt his hairy palm on the inside of her thigh. I grabbed his extending middle finger and bent it back as hard as I could. The Spaniard yelped, and his hand jerked back into the hodgepodge of packages.

"That will solve it," I said to my companion confidently. But just to be certain, I left my hand on her leg for continued protection.

For a few minutes, the only movement was the shaking of the truck as it poked towards the village, whose lights had at last become visible in the too-far distance.

Then lightly, I felt the Spaniard's rough hand touch mine with a gentle stroking.

Incredulously, I thought to myself, he thinks my hand is her hand. With the jumble inside this truck cab, he cannot tell limb from limb. Well, let him. If it will keep him occupied for another 20 minutes or so, we can reach that village.

So I suppressed my natural urge to withdraw and allowed this Spaniard to continue his attempted seduction of the misidentified hand. He turned the hand over and softly rubbed his finger in my palm. Then I suddenly felt stubble on the back of my hand as he pressed his lips to it in the most gallant of continental fashion. He licked on the top of my thumb; he sucked on the end of my ring finger, and when he acted as if he were going to move on beyond the hand, I moved my fingers to caress the bristly hair on his chin.

The Spaniard found heaven in this coy American hand which teased him by bending his finger, then excited him by sexily stroking the side of his jaw. He moved slowly with his courtship. After all, he had all night, all the way to Zaragoza.

And as for me, I took courage from the village lights growing ever closer, and whenever I questioned what the implications might be for my manhood, I tried to remember how cold it was outside.

Just when the Spaniard had done every seductive thing to my hand he could envision and was about to insist on involving some leg, the truck finally rolled into the little village.

"Hacer alto . . . aqui!" I suddenly shouted to the driver to make the truck halt, and he did. The driver probably had no idea his fellow farm worker was getting so lucky with a hand.

"No, no, Zaragoza, Zaragoza," the passenger-side Spaniard was yelling. But despite his burst of protest, my female companion and I were able to climb out of the truck on the driver's side with our knapsacks and underwear intact. As the two Spaniards argued, we ran down the narrow village streets in search of a hotel.

The experience taught me something every good editor should know: Even a hand is not always what it seems.

And somewhere in the south of Spain there is a farm worker who, to this day, believes that except for the changeable mind of some stupid young man, he would have sampled the affections of a young American woman whose hand was hotter than a chili pepper on the coldest of nights.

THE SECRET WISDOM
OF THE SECRET BALLOT

Few professions could be more consistently humbling than the one of putting out a smalltown newspaper.

If a smalltown editor misquotes a councilman and skews the angle of a council meeting story a little, the councilman tells his friends who tell their friends, and before the week is out, everyone who cares to know will know that the newspaper editor blew it again. Tsk, tsk, will that editor ever get it right?

A country editor must live among the people he covers. He sees them week in and week out at the grocery store, in the coffee shop, at church. Their wives talk over the backyard fences. Their children play on the same Little League teams.

Thus, a smalltown editor has strong motivation to be accurate and fair since he can count on his friends to point out what is wrong with the newspaper in often nauseating detail. He may be forced to admit: The reason the newspaper will publish its next edition is to apologize for what went wrong with its last edition.

This Main Street feedback, whether it comes as a joke in the barbershop or a punch in the eye at the gas station, keeps an editor grounded. Every issue of the newspaper can be a lesson in humility.

But I am not sure other professions offer the same reality-check opportunities. Being an oil well pumper, for example, seems to allow much time for dreaming and few chances to be dragged back down to earth.

I mention this profession in particular because my friend, Roy Fletcher, is a pumper, and until recently, Roy had as little contact with the actual ground as anyone I know.

A pumper spends his days going around the countryside starting, stopping, checking, repairing, and logging oil wells. A pumper is a lone eagle who seems to work at his own pace with rather loose supervision by the oil company which employs him. He always has time for a morning cup of coffee or an early afternoon beer. The job is perfect for Roy Fletcher.

But Roy was a man determined to live the American daydream. A quick mind like his shouldn't be confined to the body of an oil well pumper. He would go into politics.

The ruddy-faced Roy came bopping in the newspaper at mid-morning to tell me the news. Without slowing down, he danced past me at the front counter, sat down in the chair behind my desk, put his feet up on my wastebasket, and shared his announcement:

"I have decided to run for county commissioner," Roy stated with absolute confidence as if I had been begging him to throw in his hat. "Of course, I can count on your support."

"Well, uh, uh," I answered indecisively, "this is all a bit sudden, isn't it Roy? Why on earth would you want to run for commissioner?"

Roy spat his wad of chewing tobacco between his boots and into my wastebasket: "It's a plum job. Pays $25,000 a year and takes only two morning meetings a month. I can do that job between oil wells. And nobody knows these county roads like I do. I drive them 25,000 a year just making my regular rounds. I could watch them like a hawk."

"That you could, Roy," I admitted. "But in this state, the commissioner job always goes to some unemployed road grader driver. You've got a job."

"You sound like my old lady," Roy said as he wiped something I hoped was mud off the bottom of one of his boots and into my wastebasket. "She can think of a hundred reasons why I shouldn't make this race. But as you know, being a pumper was only something to do while I decided how best to use my talents."

"Yes," I said as I was forced to sit in the chair across from my own desk, "but your wife, Ann, is a reasonable person. And what about those screenplays you were writing?"

"Those baboons in Hollywood wouldn't recognize genius if it was bolted to their butts," Roy said as he opened every drawer of my desk and peered inside. "I have decided I am perfectly suited for a political career. You know how good I am with people."

"Yes, Roy, but can you get elected commissioner? Glenn Holderman won that post decisively and has been reelected twice already."

"Piece of cake," Roy responded. "I drive all over this precinct. I can see every voter personally. I know you don't normally endorse political candidates, but I want you to consider making an exception and throwing the weight of the newspaper behind my candidacy."

"Well, uh . . . I'll think about it."

"Good man," Roy said as he rocked out of my chair and onto his feet. And with a friendly punch into my shoulder blade, he was gone.

The least surprising thing about Roy was that he was forever surprising. He had always been that way, even when we were briefly at the same university together. He was three years younger than I was, so I was completing my senior year at college when he arrived as a freshman. Lonely and not easily accepted, Roy searched for someone from his home town and attached himself to me. To my dismay, he even moved across the street from me.

Roy's family had made a $10,000 mistake by insisting that he enroll in the university. Intelligent but unfocused,

Roy wandered among the disciplines without absorbing any of them. His family had in mind pharmacy, but Roy signed up for philosophy and psychology.

Roy seemed to really make an effort to study for his first semester exam, but when the quiz included none of the questions he had prepared to answer, he abandoned the format of the test and instead wrote a critique of the professor's teaching style. When his exam paper came back, the professor had written in red on the top: "Very interesting. F."

Roy showed the test to me with something approaching pride: "The professor said 'very interesting.' "

"He also said, 'F,' which means failing, Roy."

"He can't fail someone as creative as I am," Roy contended.

Soon Roy had earned notices of failing grades in every one of his courses, except physical education. By mid-semester, he stopped attending all classes, which meant he was always watching for me to come back to my garage apartment, and he nightly arrived on my doorstep only seconds behind me.

As he invaded my efficiency, he walked through the apartment opening every drawer, every cabinet, every closet. He inspected the kitchen, the bathroom, the bedroom, and he commented on anything that had changed since his last visit. "Why did you start putting your toothbrush in the amber glass instead of the clear one? I'll bet the clear one was always showing that gunky dried toothpaste." Only after he had examined the apartment from front window to sock drawer would he sit down and talk about his latest dream:

"I wrote today for a new Thunderbird," he said as he made himself comfortable on the college student couch which had been worn out for more than a decade.

"You did what?"

"I wrote the Ford Motor Company and asked them to send me a new Thunderbird."

"Roy, you're the guy who has to eat with me half the time because you have no money," I said. "You have no job. You can't come close to making the car payments on the allowance your father sends."

Roy swelled up like a toad. I had taken the bait. He had me. "How little you know, my pragmatic friend, about the fine art of promotion. I am not buying the Thunderbird. I am asking Ford to give me one free. In return, I have promised to drive it to every major college campus in America and show it off. Ford will get a million dollars worth of publicity for the price of one puny sportscar."

"And you think Ford will accept that offer?"

"Why wouldn't they? It's cheaper than television commercials. It's far more effective than newspaper advertising. I'll make certain their new model is seen by college kids all over the country. It's brilliant. The only reason it's never been done before is that I am the first one who thought of it."

Without the bother of having to attend classes or study, Roy was able to dream up one or two of these schemes a week, and he always seemed to move on to the next one before the last dream totally collapsed around him.

But as the end of the semester approached, Roy realized that if he failed his courses, he would not be able to continue his fantasy lifestyle under the guise of higher learning. One evening, he announced to me that he would show up in his discarded classes for the first time in ten weeks and take the finals.

"I've got all the textbooks," he contended. "I'll cram them into my head, waltz into those classrooms, and shock the professors. When I ace the finals, they won't have the nerve to fail me."

Roy was right about shocking the professors who had given him up for a dropout, but he was wrong about the rest of it. When the grades were posted, he had accumulated a rather remarkable straight F record, even in physical education.

Between semesters, he guarded the family mailbox at home and managed to intercept the university's report on his performance. In good faith, his family loaded Roy's pockets with tuition money and proudly sent him back for the spring semester. However, the college looked down on students with Roy's demonstrated academic skills, and he was banned from enrolling again. So he matriculated back into his perfect Walter Mitty world with money arriving from home and no scholastics to impede his creativity. Working furiously mostly in his mind, he concocted a prospectus for a company which would reopen abandoned copper mines he had heard about in West Texas. He sent out dozens of letters seeking investors for a television game show pilot called Cliff Notes Quiz.

While he sprawled across my swayback couch one Saturday talking about his latest vision for a new kind of bean patty sandwich which would make the hamburger obsolete, a knock at the door interrupted his most detailed explanation. Standing in the door frame was Roy's father, up from home with a form letter from the university in hand. When refunding a portion of the yearlong parking fee, the college's letter had made reference to the fact that Roy had flunked out, which came as a shock to the Fletcher family.

After three hours of stressful Fletcher family conversation in my efficiency apartment, Roy agreed to join the Navy. By nightfall, he had disappeared from my life.

Ten years later, Roy returned home with Ann, perhaps the most long-suffering woman I have known, and began pumping oil wells, a good job for someone who had spent almost two semesters near a college without earning even one credit. For a couple of years, Roy tended his wells and his family almost as if his cerebellum had at least been stabilized, but then he announced his run for commissioner.

Unlike most county candidates, Roy didn't just offer his name up on the ballot, print a few business cards to pass out, run an advertisement in the newspaper, shake a few

THE SECRET WISDOM OF THE SECRET BALLOT 73

hands. Roy obsessed over the political campaign, and bothered the whole town with it night and day.

As the week of the election arrived, Roy came bounding through the newspaper's front door beaming confidence and passing out "Commission Fletcher to be Commissioner" fliers to anyone who would accept one.

"My friend," Roy said to me as he approached, "I am going to win this election. I won't even need your newspaper endorsement. I am absolutely certain of victory."

"I don't know, Roy," I tried to caution him. "Holderman has lots of friends and family in that precinct."

"Doesn't matter," Roy said as he pushed aside the papers on my desk to make a spot where he could sit. "I have talked personally to every voter in the precinct, and I looked all of them right in the eyes and asked for their support. And all of them told me I had their votes . . . every single one. I am going to win by a landslide."

"I don't know, Roy . . ." I said lamely. "Holderman has carried this precinct three times already."

"That's ancient history," Roy declared as he sorted through my pencil holder. "I will be the new political power in this county. After I have been commissioner for a term or two, I will challenge for state representative. Then I'll run for Congress. And after that, who knows? What kind of president do you think I'd make?"

"Roy, we've been friends for years, and even I don't know what your politics are. Do you have any kind of political vision about where you would take the nation, the state, or even the county?"

"Vision . . .," Roy let the word drip off his mouth like he had puffed out a feather, "I don't need vision. Holderman has no vision for the county. The president has no vision for the country. You just don't understand politics, Mister Newspaper Editor."

Roy stood up from my desk and leaned over in my face: "Let me explain to my naive little friend." Then he walked around the newsroom as if he were already on the floor of the House of Representatives. "Politics is the art of telling people what they want to hear, plain and simple. I went all over the precinct and found out what the folks wanted to hear, and that's what I told them. And that's why I can tell you with 100 percent certainty that I will win. There will be about 3,000 votes cast in this commissioner precinct, and I know without doubt that I will get at least 80 percent of them. I expect my vote count to come in at about 2,500 at the courthouse on Tuesday night. It's a done deal."

With that, Roy cockily continued out the newspaper door and along his campaign path, while I slumped back into my chair with relief that I hadn't been forced to face the long-dreaded moment when I told him he could not have an endorsement from the newspaper.

In rural counties, election night ranks up there with the Fourth of July. All those with an interest in the politics of the county gather on the courthouse steps for the results to be posted voting precinct by voting precinct. Each new figure chalked upon the blackboard sends the old-timers into fits of interpretation about what it all means. And on this particular Tuesday night, the gathering crowd spilled off the courthouse lawn, for the ballot contained a number of good races.

With supreme confidence, Roy arrived at the courthouse and began working the crowd like a winner. After a few minutes, he noticed me sitting at the press table.

"I feel good," he said as he came over and picked up my reporter's notebook to read. "I'm going to win. This will be the start of something big."

"Good luck, Roy," I said as earnestly as I could. I supposed the county could survive even Roy's election. We'd done worse.

Then Roy suddenly turned pensive and softly whispered to me: "Mister editor, do you think it was wrong of me to vote for myself? When Ann and I went to vote today, she said it was wrong for me to vote for myself."

THE SECRET WISDOM OF THE SECRET BALLOT

"Well, I . . ." I had no idea how to respond. "I just don't know. I suppose your wife means that it's wrong from a sense of sportsmanship."

"Why the hell shouldn't I vote for myself?" Roy asked a little louder. "I'm the damn best man for the job, and I should cast my vote for the best man, now shouldn't I? This is a dog-eat-dog world, and I say to hell with those schoolboy niceties. I'm damn proud of voting for myself."

With that, he departed into the crowd once again to talk and await the returns.

If I had not previously understood the underlying wisdom of the forefathers in giving us the secret ballot, I understood after that night. I watched Roy's smile go limp and his posture crumble as the voting precinct results arrived and turned into telling white numbers on the broad blackboard. In the first box, Holderman received 439 votes. Roy got three. And so the night went.

To his credit, Roy stood there in front of the blackboard and took the punishment while Holderman posted what is believed to be the largest percentage ever garnered in a contested county race. Roy gritted his teeth, shook Holderman's hand, and wished him the best after all the results were posted. Holderman had receive 2,963 votes. Roy had gotten only 82, and most of those were probably more against Holderman than for Roy.

And to add the worst possible insult, Roy had lost his own voting precinct of his closest neighbors by a vote of 120 votes for Holderman to only one for Roy.

When it was all over, Roy shuffled over to the press table and said to me: "You know what is really bad about all this?"

I almost responded: "Because it puts the presidency out of reach?" But I didn't. Instead, I settled for a simple, "What's that, Roy."

"You notice that I lost my own voting precinct, my home area, by 120 votes for Holderman to only one for me?" Roy asked.

"Yes," I admitted, "I noticed, but your neighbors probably thought . . ."

Roy interrupted me firmly: "I'm not worried about my damn neighbors. Do you know what that one vote means?"

For a second he had lost me, and I shook my head "no."

"It means," Roy said with a look of abject rejection, "that even my wife didn't vote for me . . . even my own wife."

In all of the elections I had covered, it was the only circumstance I've ever encountered when the secret ballot was not entirely secret. And for oil well pumper Roy, it was the most humbling of possible experiences.

"Come on, Roy," I said as I put my arm around his shoulder, "Let's go drink a beer."

REGGIE THE ROCK CRITIC

Newspaper photographers are always more than a little crazy, a requirement for the job.

But Reggie was strange, even for a photographer.

Reggie was, without doubt, the sharpest dresser I ever knew, and he prided himself on the fact that his entire ensemble never cost more than five dollars.

Unlike most photographers who turn slovenliness into an art form, Reggie went on picture assignments looking like a magazine model and not at all like a cave-dwelling darkroom rat. He never strapped the cameras around his neck. They might wrinkle his ruffles. He never carried a grungy camera bag which might clash with his earth-tone tie or his chartreuse jacket.

"Like this shirt?" he would ask. "It cost me 65 cents. Like this tie? I got three like this for 50 cents at Second Chance Suits."

Reggie shopped constantly at thrift stores and used clothing outlets. He had special accounts at the Salvation Army and Goodwill Industries stores.

And everyone in town had to admit Reggie had a flair for finding colorful clothing for pennies and matching the irregular pieces into startlingly coordinated outfits. Every day, he insisted on telling me the entire cost of his ensemble piece by piece, and it never totaled more than five dollars.

As remarkably irritating as that was, it wasn't even close to his most exasperating characteristic.

You see, Reggie didn't want to be a smart-looking photographer for a community newspaper. Reggie wanted to be a rock critic for *Rolling Stone* magazine.

Without ever being asked, Reggie would tell you he knew everything there was to know about rock 'n roll music. Reggie said he knew every guitar riff Santana ever played. He alone understood the hidden dirty words behind the mumblings of Gene Vincent and the secret meaning of "Louie, Louie." He could quote the chart dates and highest chart position of every recording group from Bill Haley and the Comets to Jefferson Starship.

"Just ask me a question about rock," he pleaded with me daily. "Just ask anything . . . anything at all."

"Reggie," I responded. "I've got this newspaper to put out. I don't have time for that."

"Just ask one question, only one," Reggie begged, "so I can show you how much I know about rock music. Then you will let me write reviews."

"Reggie," I said, "this little newspaper doesn't need a rock critic. We could use another sports writer, and we are desperate for a relief copy editor, but our readers truly do not care how much you know about rock. Just try to take photographs that are in focus."

"Please, just one rock question . . . just one and that's all."

"Okay, okay, just one," I gave up. "What song can we blame for really giving birth to rock 'n roll as we have been forced to come to know it?"

Reggie ignored my sarcasm and looked at me with disdain. Such an easy question was beneath the well-dressed him, but he spit out his answer: "Rock 'n roll was truly born at Sun Records in Memphis on that day when Elvis Presley insisted on recording the Negro blues song 'That's All Right, Mama' in an upbeat style. Now ask me something hard."

To launch his career as a rock critic, the spiffy Reggie wanted to review the big name bands which roared through the area on road trips. He bugged me and bugged me about it, and he finally extracted a vague promise that he could write a review "sometime."

One day, he heard that the classic band called The Who was coming to an area venue for a one-night assault on teenage ear drums. This was his chance to have a review clip on one of the biggest groups in rock. *Rolling Stone* would see that the dandy Reggie played in the big leagues of contemporary music. This was that "sometime" I had mentioned.

After he harangued me for days, I finally gave in. What can it hurt, I told myself, to let the fashionable Reggie review The Who? After all, he did seem to know rock music, and our readers might appreciate knowing how The Who concert went.

But I cautioned him: "Be certain to call your review into the newspaper by 10:30 p.m. so it can make the morning edition." Clothing, not deadlines, was Reggie's strongest suit.

He promised he would not miss the deadline, and off he gleefully danced to become a famous rock critic.

A few minutes after 10 o'clock, Reggie called the newspaper and dictated his review over the telephone to a reporter.

"For once," I thought to myself, "Reggie is on the ball." When I read the review, it seemed okay. Reggie wrote that The Who had completely changed the direction of its music. The concert, our rock critic stated, was a departure from anything the band had done previously with a much more Southern blues style. Reggie ripped into The Who on a number of points concerning its blues technique, but hey, these were big-time professional musicians who could certainly take a little criticism.

However, the review began to draw protests as soon as the newspaper hit the stands the following morning. The telephone rang with comments like: "What on earth was your reviewer thinking?"

When the foppish Reggie drifted in, I called him into the coffee-break room and confronted him: "Reggie, we have received a dozen telephone calls complaining about your review."

"Those people just don't know rock music," Reggie answered with indignation.

I thought that could be right, so I let the matter drop for the day. But our readers didn't cast it off so easily. The following day brought a flood of letters raining on my desk. A typical letter asked: "Are you sure your reviewer was even at the concert?"

So I called Reggie back to the coffee room and went over it once again: "Reggie, were you really at that concert?"

"Why, yes, of course. Do you think I would miss The Who?"

"Then why are all of these people writing to complain about your review?" I asked as I tossed a score of letters onto the table in front of him.

The colorfully dressed Reggie slumped into the chair. He could see that he was cornered in his $4.39 outfit.

"All right, all right. I'll tell you what really happened. I had gone to the restroom when the concert actually started, and I didn't hear the opening announcement. So I assumed that the band on stage was The Who. I wrote my review and called it to the newspaper during intermission. Then I went back into the auditorium and was shocked to hear the announcement that The Who was now ready to take the stage."

'Wait, wait, wait," I said as I struggled to understand. "You reviewed the warm-up band as if it were The Who?"

"Yes, that's right," he admitted.

"But Reggie, why didn't you call back and let us kill the article?"

Reggie hung his head on his fabulous blush shirt which cost only a quarter, and he whispered: "I was ashamed to admit I couldn't tell the warm-up band from The Who."

The newspaper apologized to its readers the following day, and I suppose that was the end of Reggie the Rock Critic.

Or at least I have never seen his name in *Rolling Stone*.

But Reggie learned what every newspaper person must understand: It's better to speak up and be thought a complete fool by your editor than it is to be silent and let thousands of people know.

WHY I GAVE UP SPORTSWRITING AS A CAREER

Old editor types, such as I admit to being, can bring ourselves to consider sportswriters as "real journalists" only with neck-vein-straining difficulty.

After all, sportswriters get paid for doing what everybody else does for fun, and it is not possible to convince a man who pours concrete or loads refrigerators for a living that sportswriting is truly work.

Sportswriters often resemble little boys who never quite grew up. Instead of sweating behind the levers of a bulldozer, they go to athletic games. While their friends are raising blisters to frame a three-bedroom home, they are pecking away at a keyboard to relate their hindsight versions of what should have happened at sporting events, tasks that are not much more difficult than retelling the games over beers at the local bars.

Somehow, sportswriters have even convinced the world that the already marginal standards of journalistic objectivity must be suspended in their particular field if entertaining game stories are to be written. They get away with stating opinions, interpreting facts, second-guessing, and other shameless violations of editorial behavior that would cause news reporters to be fired.

And if that weren't already enough, sportswriters often become local celebrities as well known as the athletes they cover. Ask your average plumber who reports on the county commissioners' court, and you will see why the cliché "blank look" remains strong in the English language. But ask who covers the local sports team, and he spits out the name reflexively.

Is it any wonder, then, that most editors once aspired to become sportswriters?

In my back-shop high school years as I sweated over the casting bar to pour liquid lead into the molds called "pigs," I began to notice that otherwise grown men actually made their living going to football and baseball games and writing about them in the front shop.

That was the life for me. No more stooping while dragging 20 pounds of cotton sack through family-farm fields. No more scrubbing away layers of skin with abrasive cleanser to remove press-roller ink with its near-tatoo permanence. No more lifting or carrying or picking or pushing or sweating. I would write sports when I refused to grow up.

Unfortunately, I violated the first rule of being a commentator. To be an undisputed expert on any subject, one must first be retired from personal and active participation in that field. Otherwise, observers see him floundering about the same as everyone else, and his expertise is called into question. Have you ever seen a sportswriter who still played the game?

Not knowing the above rule and displaying my stopwatch sense of timing, I began writing a high school sports column while still a playing member of the high school football team.

The coach took my weekly pontificating on the performance of his team with the disinterest it deserved, but he must have been making mental notes as he realized he was in a unique position to strike a blow for coaches everywhere against the sportswriters of the world.

As a parenthetical matter, let me explain that I was not a football star. I was allowed to play defensive safety, not because I was a bone-crushing tackle but because I sometimes very unathletically displayed a modicum of intelligence. Unlike many of the more physically gifted players on our team, I was harder to fool with a reverse or a trick play; therefore I had some function despite limited speed, size, and strength. However, even given my proven dexterity, the rule seemed to be: "Graham is never allowed to handle the ball." I could touch the ball only when I was able to steal it from the opposing team. My own team was not allowed to throw or give it to me. Besides, I was well known as the guy with the sweating palms, not someone you want in the middle of a razzle dazzle play.

Our team had won eight games in a row, so there was little to criticize in my weekly column, but like any sportswriter worth his typewriter ribbon, I did my best. I took note one week that our play was too conservative on special teams. As an example, I cited the fact that our punt returners too frequently allowed the football to bounce deep into our own territory instead of bravely gathering in the ball and heading up field for yardage.

The coach made no comment on my column, but when the team moved a comfortable three touchdowns ahead on the following Friday night, he signaled for me as I came off the field with the defensive squad. We had stuffed the other team on three straight running plays, and they were going into punt formation at their own 30 yard line.

"Get in there and field this punt," the coach said as he shoved me back into play by the number 35 on my jersey. "I want to see how we should be doing these returns."

Stunned, I had no time to do anything but pull my helmet back on my head. It had not occurred to me that the coach would be so stupid as to think I could show him how it should be done. I was a writer. I could only tell him how to do it. He was my coach. He had seen me play. He ought to know that.

As I stood on our own 30 yard line very, very much alone, I was at once proud to be selected to touch the ball at least and apprehensive at the prospect of having to make good on my own words, an unfair position in which to place any writer.

Before I had time to consider a strategy, the sound of a foot slapping against the pigskin could be heard, and the ball lifted up over the line of scrimmage and headed in my direction.

The punt, as it turned out, was not a very good one. It slipped off the side of the kicker's shoe and had a low and short trajectory. In truth, it was the kind of punt that never should be fielded. It should be allowed to hit the ground and bounce where it would. But the thought raced through my head: "If I don't catch this punt, it will probably roll all the way to our goal, and I will have done exactly that which I had criticized."

I had no choice, I decided, but to charge the punt as hard as possible and try to grab it. Then I would head up field for a surprise touchdown, and the wisdom of my viewpoint would be illustrated for the thousands in the stands to see.

I ran forward to meet the ball before it hit the grass at about our 45-yard line. By leaning forward and outstetching my arms, I was able to get my hands on it just above the ground as I ran in full stride. My often sweating fingers grasped the ball firmly this time, and for a fraction of a second, I thought my plan might actually work.

Then as my momentum carried me forward, I felt my foot kick the ball right out of my wet palms on a dead run. The kick did not produce a little blobby dribble of a fumble as one might hope. No, the kick proved to be a line-drive blast which shot waist high between the players on both sides and rolled back even further than the original punter had stood. The shocked punter gathered his wits enough to fall on the ball on his own 15-yard line.

As the laughter in the stands reached a crescendo, I attempted to hide among our defensive squad which was coming back onto the field, but the coach was signaling for me at the sidelines. I tried to run off the field at the far end of the bench, but his waving fingers reeled me towards him.

I reached him in a state of total humiliation with chin strap resting on my number 35, but the coach just patted me on the hip pads as I went by, just as if I had made an adequate but routine play, and said without inflection of any kind: "Good punt, Graham."

To my classmates and their families in the stands, that punt-return punt will always be the athletic moment for which I am most remembered. Indeed, the game film was taken out of the can and reshown for years whenever I returned to my old high school. I can only assume that it has now been lost since the certain prize-winner has not been on one of those blooper or funny home video television shows.

But as for me, I learned an extremely valuable journalistic lesson: Never, ever tell anybody how something should be done unless there is absolutely no possibility that you could wind up doing it.

JUDGE AL AND THE CHANGE OF VENUE

Lou, a weekly newspaperman friend of mine, frequently observes: "Your friends come and go, but your enemies accumulate."

And Lou has accumulated enough enemies and been run out of enough towns that he should know. The portly editor, who was given intelligence in lieu of athletic ability, once felt compelled to abandon his automobile and run four panting miles back to the safety of the newspaper because an accumulated enemy vowed to counter a point in Lou's column with a counterpunch following the tea sipping reception at the chamber of commerce.

Lou had a particular knack for accumulating enemies. One tense deadline afternoon, the newspaper's production manager became mad enough at Lou to pronounce a "death sentence by hanging" upon the editor. The burly production manager grabbed Lou by his necktie, pulled him up under one of the low backshop ceiling fans, and poked Lou's tie in the twirling blades. Only Lou's great body weight prevented him from being hoisted from the floor and choked to death before the rest of the staff grabbed scissors and cut the tie in half, thus allowing Lou to slump to the floor and escape his own hangman's noose.

Lou's axiom often proves prophetic for those who have high-visibility dealings with the public, such as often-moving city managers, school superintendents, preachers, football coaches, and newspaper editors.

To survive, a country newspaper editor must be the most forgiving member of the community. He must always remember that the person who stands so vehemently against him on one issue will likely posture steadfastly beside him on the next. If he angers and declares persona non grata each person who disagrees with him, soon the smalltown editor will look up and see only accumulated enemies. He must treat both today's friend and today's foe with evenhandedness in the news columns without regard to what he currently thinks of each of them personally. He must not view anyone as an enemy.

While impersonal fairness is easy to say, it is not always easy to accomplish. In my experience, the biggest challenge came at the hands of County Judge Allen "Al" Carter, a politician in the great southern "good ol' boy" tradition of perpetual office holding.

Judge Al had declared himself an accumulated enemy of the newspaper three decades before I arrived in town. In fact, he had built his career on being an opponent of the newspaper, not a bad strategy for a judge in a county with a large population of dirt-floor poor, nearly illiterate voting citizens.

On only my second day in town, Judge Al saw me walking along the town square and hailed me from the courthouse steps.

"Hey you!" Judge Al yelled. "You, yes you. Aren't you the new editor?"

I confessed and walked over to talk with him.

"Hey, mister new editor," the old judge said in a cordial tone. "I can save us both a lot of time. No comment."

"Wha . . . what?" I stammered. The judge had caught me off guard. "You are County Judge Allen Carter, right?"

"You've heard about me already?" the judge almost smiled.

"You, judge, are legendary in these parts," I admitted. "I had heard of Judge Al before I even moved to town."

JUDGE AL AND THE CHANGE OF VENUE 91

The judge could not restrain himself and broke out in one of those toothy redneck grins: "Legendary, huh. That's a good word, legendary. Hey, I like that word. It means something good."

"Well, perhaps legendary is a bit strong," I said. To myself, I thought: "I should have said infamous."

"No," he disagreed, "that legendary thing will do. Hey, write that in the newspaper." Then he reached into his back pocket and produced a worn-out bulging billfold thick enough to be causing a calcium deposit the size of a baseball on his hip bone. From this packed wallet, he adroitly removed a small laminated newspaper clipping. "Here, read this."

I took the yellowed clipping encased in aging plastic and held it up to sunlight. The clipping was dated March 17, 1947, and it was a retraction for some error in a story which the newspaper had written about the county judge. It concluded with the standard: "This newspaper wishes to apologize to Judge Allen Carter for any inconvenience the article may have caused him."

I handed the clipping back to the judge: "A correction from 1947?"

Judge Al nodded. "I carry it with me to prove that your newspaper is against me." He warmly read the part he liked best: "This newspaper wishes to apologize to Judge Allen Carter for any inconvenience the article may have caused him."

"But judge," I protested, "that was three decades ago. You've carried that clipping in your wallet ever since?"

"Every day of my life," the judge said proudly. "Hey, I take it out every time your newspaper does something against me, which is all the time."

"But judge," I tried again, "I am a new editor, and I know nothing of what has happened in the past. Let us start anew, and let bygones be bygones. I will treat you with respect and fairness, and you . . . . ."

The judge would have no pabulum-like homily from some green editor who didn't know how the game was played. He interrupted: "Hey, you editors are all alike. You will come to me and want to ask about this and that. I can save us both a lot of time and trouble: No comment."

"No comment?" I still couldn't follow him. "No comment on what?"

"No comment to anything. No comment to everything," the judge stated flatly. "I give you my 'no comment' now, and you can use it whenever you feel a stupid urge to call me on the phone and ask me some dumb question you say the public has some right to know. Hey, if the public needs to know anything, I will tell them personally. In the newspaper, my only comment is no comment."

"Let me get this straight," I said as the implications of what he conveyed began to sink into my astonished brain. "You are the county judge, and no matter what question I put to you, the only thing you will say to me is . . . no comment?"

"Now you're catching on, boy," the judge said as he slapped my back in his friendly manner. "Hey, nothing personal. That's what I say to the newspaper: No comment."

"Even if I am only asking the time of the county commissioners' court meeting?"

"No comment."

"Even if I ask if the sun will rise in the east tomorrow?"

"No comment," he said, "and you can print that." With another big smile, he turned and climbed the steps back into his courthouse domain.

Novice that I was, I thought it possible that the judge pulled on my leg a little. I could not understand how a county judge could be reelected term after term and say nothing but "no comment" to the local newspaper. But I had underestimated the political skills of Judge Al. After I had collected a reporter's notebook of "no comments" from him, I began to understand the strategy behind his lack of response.

JUDGE AL AND THE CHANGE OF VENUE

Judge Al started out in life as a third-rate used car salesman, a position which allowed him to become friends with what the politically correct would now call the economically disadvantaged of the county. He financed every old junker he sold, and he made more money out of the eternal interest payments that he did from selling cars. Honest Al would let his clients stretch out their payments to forever. He even encouraged it.

A pricey public relations analyst might not recognize Al's loan list as a political base, but Al did. Soon he was loan sharking from his used car lot with little pretense of selling automobiles. The majority of the county lived hand-to-mouth, and whenever they encountered some extra expense, they borrowed the money from Honest Al. They got accustomed to owing Honest Al and paying him something every month. Al loved the concept of usury, but he also had the ability to ascertain just how much blood could be squeezed from his turnip clients.

Thus, he became known as a friend to the county's large underclass. And thus, he decided he could be elected county judge, and to the dismay of the town's stainless citizenry, he was voted in rather decisively.

"Judge Al" conveys an even more virtuous image than "Honest Al," the new county judge realized, so he closed what little remained of his junk car lot and moved his bargain finance business into the county judge's chambers of the courthouse where he had operated for decades since.

The county judge deal proved even better than he had expected. Once he came to understand the power that the office possessed, Judge Al entrenched himself through a combination of political favors granted and political favors owed him. He blatantly used the county's resources to his personal political benefit. The county hospital became his own private admitting and debt-forgiveness institution. "Sure, I'm getting your mom put in the hospital, and, hey, don't worry about the charges," he said constantly. He forced county road graders to plow down every private lane which led to a slap-wood cabin or a tireless trailer house. Most of the time, it was difficult to determine if Judge Al was displaying human kindness or political cunning, or both.

For a few years, Judge Al's election might have been said to represent a certain amount of poetic justice. After all, prior to his victory, only the well-to-do in the county could have their private roads reworked by county equipment. Now anyone qualified to vote could grab a scrap of the spoils.

The problem was that, after a couple of decades of Judge Al's rule, the spoils were gone. County government was broke, reducing services every year, and operating far into the red. The county hospital teetered at the edge of bankruptcy, and no one knew what the county would do when the debtors claimed the town's only medical facility.

By the time I arrived in town, any person with a modicum of knowledge about the community realized how desperately the county needed to rid itself of Judge Al, but the judge cut down anyone who climbed into the political ring to oppose him like Joe Louis in his prime. He had knocked out three truly respectable candidates fielded by the responsible business community with two-to-one margins, and no worthy opponent could be found to face him.

Quickly, I came to appreciate that his country bumpkin judge's posture hid a clever and perhaps even diabolical personality that, while uneducated, knew precisely what it was doing.

Like the old duck hunter adage, Judge Al believed in shooting at everything that flies and claiming everything that falls. Whenever the U.S. government would adjust Social Security payments upward for inflation, the judge would abandon the courthouse for three days and visit almost everyone in the county who drew these government checks. He would say:

JUDGE AL AND THE CHANGE OF VENUE

"Hey, Aunt Mary, I was able to get you a little increase in your Social Security. You should see your April check a bit higher. It's not a lot, but it's the best I could do for you. I'll keep trying."

And Aunt Mary would say: "Oh, thank you, thank you, Judge Al. Every little bit helps. I just don't know what we would do without you."

Judge Al delighted in making sure everybody for counties around knew that he was the poor man's county judge. He had an Archie Bunker's "whatever" command of English which kept all the lawyers laughing in their offices and the votes pouring into their election boxes. County court often was a laugh riot. Judge Al referred to a couch in sections as a "sexual couch," and he insisted on calling the place where two streets crossed an "intercourse."

"You go down to that first intercourse," he gave directions to an out-of-town attorney, "then you turn left and go through two more intercourses. Be sure to stop at the fourth intercourse."

"I always do, judge," the lawyer answered as he cracked up.

Once a polished attorney from a nearby metropolitan area requested that Judge Al grant him a change of venue.

To the amazement of the attorney and the amusement of everyone else, Judge Al responded:

"Now listen here, mister big city lawyer, if you're going to start throwing around those fancy legal terms in my courtroom, I'm just going to have to move this trial over to the city where they use those big words."

And when our newspaper printed stories like "Judge Al and the Change of Venue," the judge feigned anger, but I came to realize that he secretly loved it. The newspaper played right into his hands, and he played the newspaper as easily as a Calypso bongo in Trinidad.

"See, what'd I tell you," I would hear him saying to the courthouse bench sitters. "That newspaper never misses a chance to print something stupid that I do. But it won't run anything that I tell them. Hey, that newspaper has always been out to get me." And he would pull out his clipping from 1947 as proof.

Slowly, I understood the defense strategy he had designed to thwart the truth. When the newspaper ran a story about the pending bankruptcy of the county hospital, all the explanation we could include from the county judge was his standing "no comment."

Then he would walk around town complaining that he could explain it all, but the newspaper wouldn't let him have any space to do so.

When the newspaper uncovered a corruption story about county equipment, materials, and workers being used to build Judge Al a new barn, we would be obliged to include his traditional "no comment."

"Hey, now hey, guys," Judge Al told his cronies, 'I called that newspaper, and I told that editor why that story was all wrong, but did you see what he printed? Did you see what he did to me? He ignored everything I said to him and only printed another of those 'no comments' he always sticks in stories about me. Hey, I ask you guys, have you ever known me not to comment? Hey, I'm the talkingest dude in this county. 'No comment,' my foot."

The judge's listening audience would nod in agreement. He was the "talkingest dude in the county," and they could never visualize him saying "no comment."

As an editor, the judge's posture began to drive me crazy. How could I treat him fairly when his entire defense depended upon the perception that he was being treated unfairly by the newspaper? How could the citizenry make an informed decision about this county judge when we appeared to be unfair to him no matter what facts we uncovered? He had the newspaper right where he wanted us.

I became obsessed with finding a way to force Judge Al to make any statement other than "no comment," but even the tightest corner we backed him into did not alter his strategy. I explained in my column why "no comment" always appeared as the only comment from Judge Al. I even ran a big blank space in the newspaper which we labeled as a spot reserved for Judge Allen Carter to make any response to any story which appeared. The paragraph at the top of the big white empty spot said Judge Al could fill the space anytime he liked with anything he wanted. But nothing worked.

"No comment," Judge Al always continued to say to me. Then he grinned because we knew he had me once again. And the judge's great wealth kept growing, while his county slipped into financial ruin.

However, every suit of armor, no matter how carefully crafted, has its chink. One day, the newspaper's young reporter stumbled across a crack in Judge Al's stonewall protection, and the reporter was bright enough to recognize it. The county judge's duties included the probation of estates where the individual died "intestate," or without a will. The reporter crosschecked and discovered that Judge Al had wound up owning several of the pieces of land which had passed through his court.

We picked one plot of 30 acres on the north edge of town and tried to trace the family members of the poor man who died leaving no will. It took weeks of effort, time that's hard to come by in a small-town newspaper, but our reporters finally located two sisters of the deceased man living in the worst slums of Dallas. The two elderly sisters, one of whom was struggling with cancer, told us how nice Judge Al had been to give them $10,000 for that 30 acres. The judge told them:

"Hey, that old piece of land your brother had isn't worth anything. Can't grow nothing on it. Back taxes owed just about eat up the value. But I can see you two sisters need the money so very badly, so out of the goodness of my heart, I'm going to give you $10,000 for it. I know I shouldn't pay ten. Hey, it's not worth more than $200 an acre. That would be $6,000. And those back taxes . . . oh my. But I'll give you ten because you-all need it so much."

The sisters trusted Judge Al. They took the $10,000. The judge probated the will and took title to the land.

Six months later, Judge Al sold the 30 acres for $300,000.

When the newspaper hired a surveyor to determine precisely just where this plot of land was located, we found ourselves looking at the 20-store Bentwood Shopping Center.

Some stories have repercussions like an earthquake, and this was one of those. The tremors and aftershocks could be felt going out in all directions from the newspaper. The judge had cheated two elderly women, one near death with cancer, out of their inheritance, and his underprivileged constituency could not tolerate that. The title company, based on the judge's court actions, had given a guarantee on the ownership of the land which was clearly in jeopardy. And local investors had sunk hundreds of thousands of dollars into the land and its development. Retailing companies had put hundreds of thousands more into building a grocery store, a discount store, and rows of strip-center shops. With all this at risk, the state's Judicial Qualifications Committee could no longer keep its feet upon its comfortable desks, and a state probe was launched.

Very shortly, I learned that Judge Al was ready to make a statement. When we arrived at his combination judge and loan office at the courthouse, Honest Al was packing his things in boxes and said he had only two words to say.

"No comment?" I asked.

"Hey, no," he said sadly. "The two words are: I resign."

After 30 years, the citizens of the county had finally gotten the change of venue they needed from Judge Al.

THE BALLOON LADY OF DUBLIN

"Deadline" is a magic word.

If a newspaper person says, "I'm on deadline," the non-newspaper person may not know exactly what that means in terms of production and timetables but is aware that the deadline excuses any abruptness. A deadline is inviolate.

I must confess that most of us newspaper-types find that word "deadline" very useful, and we call on it far more than is actually necessary.

When Mrs. Ancil Jones corners me and begins to retell the entire program of the county's genealogical society, I admit I often say: "That's very interesting, Mrs. Jones, and I'd love to hear every single word. However, I'm on deadline."

Of course, she backs off immediately: "Oh, I'm sorry. I didn't realize you were on a deadline this early in the morning." And she stops what would otherwise be a fifteen-minute recounting in mid-sentence.

However, I can recall one night when the magic word had no potency for one of our readers. The time was approaching 9:30 p.m. on one of those summer Saturdays when it never seems to grow dark, and it was nearing that bewitching moment when the Sunday newspaper had to "go to bed," which is printer talk for the pages being placed on what was once the flat surface of the old letterpress. At this time I really was "on deadline."

I was running a few minutes late that night, and I had the staff hustling to make up the time when composing room foreman Jose came into the newsroom.

"I've got a hysterical woman calling for the editor back on our production line," Jose said.

I never looked up: "I'm in the throes of wrapping this paper up, Jose. Tell her to call back in 30 minutes on the editorial line. Tell her I'm on deadline."

Jose disappeared into the backshop of the newspaper, but he returned seconds later: "The woman is screaming that it's an emergency. She has to talk with the editor right now."

"Oh, all right," I yielded as I tossed my editing pencil down. "I'll talk to her. This will probably make us miss the Stephenville mail truck."

Normally, my policy was to talk to anybody who called without asking who it was or what they wanted. As an old editor once noted to me: "Why do you ask who it is when you are going to talk to everybody anyway?"

Why indeed? Ask not for whom the phone bell tolls. It tolls for the community newspaper editor. So I quit asking who was calling, and I no longer allowed our receptionist to inquire.

In every newspaper, a familiar cry is some version of this: "Nut call on line two."

But even the so-called "nuts" of the town often know things the newspaper needs to learn, so we talk to anybody, anytime.

Besides, I trusted Jose's judgment, perhaps even more than my own. The production of the newspaper on time was uppermost in Jose's mind, and if that caller could convince efficient but always pressed Jose that the editor should be interrupted on deadline, the editor most likely should go to the telephone.

I threaded my way through the composing room to the telephone which hung on the rear wall.

"This is the editor," I said into the telephone's speaker.

"Oh, thank God," a woman cried. "Help me, help me. What are we going to do?"

"Do about what?"

She was indignant: "Don't tell me you don't know. You've got to help me."

"Know about what?"

"The red things. The red dots. The red balloon things are everywhere. Don't try to tell me you haven't received dozens of calls."

"Actually," I said, "yours is the first. And I am right this second on deadline. If you can give me your telephone number, I will call you back in 30 minutes, or I can have a reporter contact you tomorrow."

"Tomorrow?" Now I had really made her angry. "Don't you understand. There won't be any tomorrow."

"But I can save you long-distance call time."

"Forget that," she wept, "none of us will be around for the next telephone billing. Listen, you stupid editor, don't hang up on me. I am calling from my hall closet where the red things have chased my grandson and me. They are trying to get in the door right now. We may be gone at any moment. Isn't that right, Jimmy?"

I could hear a whimpering Jimmy confirm her statement in the background. I tried for facts: "Just what is it that is endangering you?"

"You mean, you're not under attack too?"

"No, all is quiet here at the newspaper office. Nothing unusual reported on this hot summer Saturday night."

"I don't believe you. As far as I can see on the horizon are these red dots as big as basketballs or beach balls. They are coming down from the sky, hundreds of them, thousands of them, hundreds of thousands of them, everywhere. My grandson and I were rocking in the porch swing when the balloons began to float toward us from all over. They cover the neighbor's house. They are flooding all of the countryside. They must be coming down even over on Dublin. They chased us into the house. Then they began coming in through the screen door, and they drove us into the closet. I don't think we can hold out much longer. This is the end of the world." She broke down in a shattered voice, and the sounds of an older woman and a young boy crying were all I could hear.

As I talked to her, I signaled Jose to go into the newsroom and manhandle a reporter back to this telephone.

"Don't worry," I told her. "The newspaper will take care of this. We'll find out what is happening, and we will send someone to rescue you."

"Oh, thank God, thank God," she said. "What are these things, and why are they coming down on my house? You must have had other reports."

"None," I assured her calmly. "This is the first we've heard about the red things."

When reporter Kerry arrived at the composing room phone, I briefed him on the woman's predicament, and I asked him to get any solid information he could from her while staying on the line.

After Kerry took the phone, I went back to the newsroom and put the rest of the staff to work trying to confirm the unconfirmable. One reporter checked the weather bureau, the Air Force, the airport, the police station, and other official sources. But she found no other unusual happenings.

Another reporter called the sheriff's office at Dublin. Again, the dispatcher was experiencing only a humid summer night with no excitement except for the teenagers hotrodding up and down Main Street. Who was this woman? She lived outside of Dublin, but as far as anybody knew, she was an upstanding, churchgoing member of the community with no drinking problem previously noted. She was not a person who ever called the sheriff's office or whom the deputies ever called. Hers was not a house any of the law officers had visited because of a disturbance. But the sheriff's office promised to send a unit to check it out.

Reporter Kerry took several pages of notes, and he promised to journey to Dublin and visit the caller early the following morning. The woman finally hung up the telephone without notice, and attempts to call her back were unsuccessful.

Obviously, there is nothing a newspaper can run about this kind of story, so we went to press without any notification about the invasion of the red balloons in the Dublin peanut farm country.

The following day, Kerry visited the woman, but she would not open the door or say anything to him. Nor had she been willing to talk to the deputies.

And just what combination of atmospheric or medicinal conditions caused the red balloons of Dublin, I never knew.

THE STAR OF THE POLICE SCANNER

The background music for the life story of a country editor would most appropriately be the squelch of the police scanner.

This noisy sound track plays as endlessly as an air-conditioning unit in most small newspapers, and editors, like law-enforcement officers, learn to listen only subconsciously until something about the scanner's intensity level awakens awareness.

As a squelch-immersed editor, the most difficult adjustment was the acceptance that my wife, Kathryn, was by her nature destined to be the star of the police scanner.

Whenever the police radios whined that officers were responding to some odd accident, I came to accept that the subject of any truly bizarre calamity was likely to be Kathryn. And if the entire news and advertising staff stood up following a scanner announcement and said in unison, "Wow, did you hear that? Some loony bird just fell down the hospital laundry chute . . . all three floors into the basement," I knew without inquiry it had to be Kathryn.

Who else could tumble backwards out of a bathroom sink while trying to wash both feet at once?

Who else would insist on trying for a pilot's license even though she was totally blind in one eye? (When the agent of the Federal Aviation Administration showed up on our doorstep and insisted on tearing up Kathryn's beginner pilot papers in front of our eyes, it almost restored my faith in government.)

Who else could go into full emergency-room labor and give birth to an intrauterine device?

In fairness, I must say that none of this is Kathryn's fault. As a young teenager, she contracted encephalitis and went into a coma for several weeks. When she miraculously regained consciousness, her muscles had atrophied, and she was blind. Slowly and courageously, she fought to return to what she tries to pass off as a normal lifestyle with sight in one eye and with limited coordination. She cannot help that doors and walls leap out in front of her, that roads curve without warning, that even an unlevel sidewalk crack can cause her to kiss concrete.

Even though I knew Kathryn's medical background, I didn't understand the implications it all had for a struggling young editor who was trying to raise a family in something as accident-provoking as a mobile home, which back then we called a "trailer house." I blissfully went off to do editorial war with the important world of news thinking that little of consequence could happen on the home front. I had not yet learned to ignore the clicking and clacking of high-toned stories which flowed out of Washington, D.C., and into our Associated Press teletype machine, and instead keep my ear open to the police scanner so I could know what Kathryn was up to at the house.

When the fire department reported over the air late one morning that it was responding to a stove-top grease fire at the town's southwest-side mobile home park, I had some concern since we lived in the place along with dozens of other trailer families. It was almost lunch time anyway, so as quickly as I could, I wrapped up what I was doing and followed the fire truck. Unfortunately, I was about ten minutes behind. In later and more experienced years, I would have known that any slightly unusual police scanner call meant rush home to Kathryn.

Kathryn had made two risky decisions at the same time: One, she had decided to fry hamburger steak patties in the skillet for lunch; and two, she had left two-year-old daughter Amy inside the trailer for two seconds while she went five steps outside to the trash can. Of course, when she returned from the trash and pulled on the door to the trailer house to get back in, little Amy had thrown the latch and locked it.

An adventuresome child who ate anything her hands could pick up (even the knobs off the television set), Amy had discovered that it was easy to flip the door latch to "lock."

Kathryn pounded on the door and peered in the window at the little redhead playing inside: "Amy, darling, now you must turn the latch back the other way . . . Amy, unlock the door for Mommy . . . Amy, lift that little latch on the door . . . you know that little latch . . . I'll let you eat a nice radio knob. . . ."

Amy tried to follow her mother's instructions, but she had just learned to lock the door. Unlocking was still several weeks away.

As Kathryn yelled through the door at her daughter, she saw smoke seeping around the edges and realized that the hamburger patties were now burning on the stove. The grease could easily burst into flame, and the trailer house could incinerate like a penny box of matches.

With panic shivers running through her body, Kathryn suddenly became desperate to regain entry to the trailer. She leaped off the platform porch and dashed around to the front of the trailer. She climbed upon the trailer's long iron tongue to reach the front jalousie window, which she found slightly opened but with hamburger patty smoke pouring out.

The window was hinged at the top and opened from the bottom. By pulling out on it, Kathryn was able to force the window up just enough to give her a crawl space of about twelve smoky inches through which she was determined to climb. She poked the screen wire back into the trailer and tried to squeeze her body through the foot-wide opening. Her head and shoulders penetrated the grease-smoked trailer interior, and she pulled herself inside as far as her waist.

But Kathryn's rear end was too big for the crawl space, and it stuck in the window as the jalousie clamped down on her. As any farmer knows, two pounds of sausage won't go into a one-pound skin.

Gasping inside the cloudy trailer interior, Kathryn was lodged tight. She could not pull herself through to the inside of the trailer, and the jalousie window would not allow her to retreat to the outside. So she could do little but hang in the window while the hamburger patties fried them all to hell.

Kathryn's panic-infected daughter began crying at her highest decibels inside the foggy trailer. Amy ran to her dangling mother and grabbed on to her neck in fear. Kathryn tried to force the little arms to let go, but Amy grasped as tight as a johnson grass tick. Both were swinging inside the window, choking and coughing in a trailer house black with smoke and perhaps ready to burst into open flame.

"Ding dong. Avon calling."

Kathryn heard the doorbell ring. Someone to help me, she thought, so she yelled: "Help! Help! Come around to the front of the trailer. Please, come around to the front."

Kathryn listened to the sound of someone stepping off the platform porch and walking around to the front of the trailer. A voice spoke to Kathryn's posterior as it stuck out of the front window:

"Hello, I'm your Avon lady," the voice said cheerfully to Kathryn's rump with no hint that this was anything other than a routine sales call.

Is she accustomed to talking to her customers' fannies, Kathryn thought, but instead of commenting upon the conversation, she had the sense to scream: "Help! The trailer's on fire, my little girl is inside, and I'm stuck in this window. Call the fire department!"

The Avon lady rushed away and did just that, but Avon never came calling on this particular trailer house again.

With sirens screeching through the otherwise calm summer day, the vigilant volunteer firemen arrived on the scene. With adrenalin-driven axes, they smashed through the trailer's door and left it crumpled upon the ground behind the porch. They pried little Amy from her mother's stretching neck, and they doused every inch of the trailer house in about two feet of water.

While two firemen pushed up on the window until it broke, the volunteer captain tugged on Kathryn's buttocks until they both sprawled backwards into the trailer tongue.

Within only a couple of minutes, the fire in the frying pan was out. Kathryn was freed. Amy was rescued. The trailer was destroyed.

And just as quickly as they came, the firemen were gone.

I met the fire truck coming back, and I thought to myself: "They can't have put out a fire already. It must have been a false alarm."

As I walked up to our trailer house, I could see Kathryn sitting outside on the platform porch, and I cheerfully sang out the salutation: "Hello, honey. Did you have a nice morning?"

She looked up at me with fire in her eyes.

I still didn't get it, so I tried another greeting: "What's for lunch?"

"Beef jerky," she said without a smile.

SPINNING A YARN, SPINNING A TRUTH

No chasm, not even the Grand Canyon, can be as wide as the gap between what is true and what is told-as-true.

A newspaper editor must precariously make his way across the flimsy rope bridge from told-as-true to true very often. And he frequently must bear the wrath of community critics for not writing what they claim to know for absolute certain to be a fact.

"That editor is clearly covering up for the powers-that-be once again."

In my more idealistic and controversial youth, I managed to be invited to newspaper elsewhere with some degree of regularity, and after I had searched for that "truth and justice thing" in a number of different small towns, I began to notice striking similarities about what always is told-as-true.

In each new town, some small group whispered me aside to provide "background" on the real story of the community. As soon as the furtive spokesman began to talk, that deja vu feeling fought its way forward into my consciousness. I had heard this tale before in every other town in which I had newspapered.

Soon, I found myself numbering these rumors in my mind as myths one through ten, and I made a mental game of seeing how quickly in the story I would be able to recognize the myth. Usually, no more than 20 or 30 words were required to see the pattern emerging. The most common rumors were:

Myth One: The "We Ran Off General Motors" Rumor.

Every town in which I have lived has a story which goes something like this: Years ago, General Motors (or some other giant company) visited the town and wanted to relocate its entire Detroit operations here. It would have made this town bigger than Dallas. But the powers-that-be didn't want the town to grow, so they ran off General Motors.

When this story was examined for truth, it didn't stand up any better than a spineless broomstick scarecrow. Occasionally, it turned out that a big company like General Motors once did pass through the town looking for a plant site, but the company also passed through scores of other towns before selecting a location which had nothing to do with the powers-that-be. A grain of truth perhaps, but I have never known this most common of all myths to actually be true.

Myth Two: The "He Gets His Money From Drug-Running" Rumor.

The number of times this rumor has been told-as-true to me is truly staggering. For every smalltown citizen who has done well for himself, there is an underground tidbit passed around the community that he is dealing drugs.

The rumor is particularly persistent if the relatively well-to-do citizen has gotten his money from investments or inheritance or any other method not clearly visible to his fellow small town residents. If every one of these stories were true, this country would have more drug kingpins than we have convenience stores, and I don't believe that is economically possible. So I never believed that the town's most prominent businessman was the "real power behind the Colombian cartel" until the feds swooped down and arrested him, which never seemed to happen.

A similar myth is the "that business is nothing but a front for organized crime" rumor. This piece of gossip is often tossed around but is almost never true. However, in every town, there was someone who took me on a tour and pointed out this store and that store as Mafia-controlled. Could the Mafia really operate that many doughnut outlets?

Myth Three: The "Disneyland Is Coming" Rumor.

Perhaps the most pervasive rumor in almost every small town in America is that one which contends the Disney people from California have taken an option on a piece of land near town, and the community is about to become the next Disneyland, Disneyworld, or Disneydesert. Never mind that the town is 200 miles from any population center, 100 miles from the nearest four-lane highway, and surrounded by undrained swamp land. No matter how many denials the poor besieged Disney people issue in Anaheim, the rumor lives on, fueled mostly by the eternal hope of real estate development.

Myth Four: The "Coffee Mafia Runs the Town" Rumor.

Almost every small town has several groups of people who gather informally for a cup of early morning or mid-morning coffee, and this seems to feed the myth which always goes something like this: Six powerful people meet secretly at 7 a.m. each Monday and decide what will be allowed to happen in the town that week. Sometimes a community critic will even name the six powerful people who control every single aspect of life in the little city.

I always wanted to be present at one of these coffees, but I never found one that even came close to living up to the ever-present rumor. Usually, I personally knew that at least half of the people fingered as the Town's Coffee Mafia wouldn't even speak to each other, much less agree on everything.

The fact that there was never one smudged fingerprint of evidence to support any of these rumors failed to slow them down very much, and even when I exposed a rumor such as "Disneyland is coming" to the hard, cold reality of black ink, one of the town's real estate agents still came in two weeks later and slipped me an aside:

"Listen, I've got a high-placed friend in the state capitol who told me for a fact that he had seen the Disney application to convert that old industrial waste dump south of town into a new theme park. I'm telling you this in strictest confidence. You can't print it yet, but it will happen. You can put that in your pipe and smoke it."

Smoke is what the story always turned out to be.

In little communities, everybody minds everybody else's business, or at least tries to. And the attribute of watching out for the neighbor which is so helpful in times of trouble or stress can be so unfair when the trait becomes gossip, perhaps the most unpleasant part of small town life.

A newspaper assumes an obligation to sort the true from the told-as-true, particularly if the story going around is one which has deep implications for the well-being of the community.

So even though I was skeptical, I listened to rumors that the state's biggest illicit methamphetamine laboratory had been set up somewhere in the county's numerous wooded areas. The lab, as the story went, was being protected by Sheriff Harold Lubitsch Jr. The newspaper kept receiving calls, mostly anonymous, which repeated this told-as-true tale.

That a methamphetamine lab had been set up in our quiet little county was not unbelievable. Others had been previously. But that Sheriff Harold Junior could be involved strained the imagination.

Harold Junior lived all of his life on the small Lubitsch family farm three miles west of town, and he came from impeccably honest and hardworking German stock. His father, Harold Senior, was so truthful he would detail every weakness in his Holstein cow before he sold it to you. And the price must always be what Harold Senior considered fair, not too high, not too low.

Harold Junior started life as a typical ruddy, freckle-necked boy, but when he reached high school, he couldn't stop growing up. By his junior year, he was an unexpected six foot, six inches tall, and as he filled out to 240 pounds, Harold Junior was imposing as tight end on the football team, post on the basketball team, state-caliber high hurdler, and just the kind of menacing companion you wanted walking beside you across the opposing team's parking lot. With red-haired temper, Harold Junior found frequent occasion to display his strength through fisticuffs. Rare was the athletic competition which didn't involve Harold Junior's scheduling a fight for after the game.

The townsfolk worried that Harold Junior might be too overflowing with testosterone to stay out of the state prison, but Harold Junior somehow made it through his knuckle-bashed teenage years, and off he went to the university in the fall on a football scholarship.

By spring, Harold Junior quietly returned home with the plausible explanation: "If I stayed at that college until the millennium, I would never, ever make the slightest bit of sense out of algebra."

Harold Junior went back to the family land, but his younger future-farmer brother had already staked out the role of heir apparent to the agriculture father. After four years, Harold Junior realized the family would fare better if he earned his living elsewhere, and he signed on to wear the badge as a deputy.

By all accounts, he was a good one. His rounder reputation fit quite naturally in a deputy's uniform. As a youth, he had already whipped almost everyone in the county who needed whipping. His size alone was enough to sober up the most undomestic of disturbances when he arrived on the scene. And when the old sheriff retired, Harold Junior ran to replace him and was handily elected over several older and more experienced candidates.

Harold Junior carefully preserved his athletic bloody-nosed persona even as he approached the age of 40. He still played in the alumni football and basketball games. He still rode bulls in the annual roundup rodeo. He still implied that he would fight at the drop of a Stetson. All of these images were useful in law enforcement.

Some rumors about the bachelor sheriff could have had a ring of truth, but Harold Junior involved in illegal drug manufacturing? I thought it most unlikely.

And yet, the stories persisted.

I was ordering a large lemonade one hot August afternoon at the outside window of the Dairy Queen when Amos Blackmon signaled me over to his car.

"Get in," he said under his breath as if there were some emergency. "I've got something shocking, very shocking to tell you. It's going to put this county on its ear."

News media types are always talking about a "reliable source." From checking out things Amos told me previously, I knew him to be a "mostly unreliable source," but a good editor must always listen. Amos usually had a speck of truth among his cow patty of information. Sometimes a tiny portion of what he dumped on me would actually prove true.

As I sat in the passenger side of his Dodge Ram pickup, Amos spooned two bites of his soft Dairy Queen ice cream and said: "This is so terrible that I don't know how to begin. . . ."

"Just tell me, Amos," I pleaded.

"Sheriff Harold Junior is running a methamphetamine lab out in the county," he said as if sharing the secret of the atomic bomb.

"Oh that rumor," I laughed. "Amos, I've been hearing that for weeks, but I cannot find one fact to substantiate it."

Amos was indignant that I had not fallen into rapture over his tip: "Then just where does Harold Junior go every Thursday afternoon? He disappears every Thursday right after lunch and never comes back until Friday morning. Don't you think that's strange?"

"Amos, just because the man takes an occasional afternoon off . . ."

"Occasional, my sore toe," Amos countered. "He is in a secret meeting with the drug lords every Thursday afternoon. I know people who have seen him driving into the woods at the far northeast end of the county on Thursday afternoon, and he stayed in there for hours and hours. Now why would a sheriff do something like that if he wasn't protecting a drug operation?"

"I don't know, Amos," I said. "There could be lots of reasons."

"And," Amos said as he gulped down another glob of ice cream, "there could be one reason: Drug money. Just check it out, will you?"

"I don't know, Amos. That's not much to go on . . ."

"You are the newspaper editor," he reminded me pointlessly. "It's your duty to fight crime and corruption in this county."

"Okay, okay, Amos," I conceded. "I will poke around a little and see what I can find."

I knew Sheriff Harold Junior well enough to doubt that he would be involved in anything worse than an occasional Friday night of gambling with the boys, but it was true that he was never available at the sheriff's office on Thursday afternoon. And he wasn't out playing golf, or anywhere else he could be reached.

So I decided to trail him on a Thursday afternoon to see just where he went. If journalism school taught a course in undercover detective work, I missed taking it. I knew next to nothing about following someone, especially not a trained law enforcement officer.

And it went just like you might expect. When Harold Junior climbed in his county vehicle and departed the sheriff's office, I poked along behind him through the city streets, out the highway north of town, down the farm-to-market pavement to the east, and to the dirt county road which disappeared into the forest. I tried to keep Harold Junior's car in sight without being close enough to be noticed.

But immediately after the sheriff turned off on the county road, he halted his vehicle behind a clump of cedar bushes. Not realizing that he had stopped, I turned onto the road and suddenly found my car braking at his back bumper. The tall reddish frame of Harold Junior half sat, half leaned on the trunk of his car.

"Why are you following me?" he asked with point blank seriousness.

"Well, uh . . . uh . . .," I said as I got out of my car and walked up to him. "I guess there's nothing to do but to ask outright: The rumors in the county are you meet with the drug lords every week. Just where do you go each Thursday afternoon?"

The lanky sheriff's frame slumped with laughter. "Is that all? Well, get back into your car and follow me."

Sheriff Harold Junior blazed a trail through the curving county road until he came to a sprawling resort cabin. As our two cars approached, a slender young man came out to greet us.

"Harold," he said with interest, "just who is this you have brought with you?"

"He's only a newspaper editor who wanted to know what I do every Thursday afternoon," Harold Junior said. "I thought I would show him our weaving club."

"Weaving club?" I was stunned.

"Yes," Harold Junior said as he opened the cabin door and led me into a room where a group of men were working with cloth bolts, looms, and spinning wheels. "A group of us who like weaving meet up here every Thursday afternoon. We make fabrics. See, look at this one I've been working on for months." The sheriff unfolded a bulk of brightly colored material.

"Wait, now wait a minute," I said. "You mean you come here every Thursday afternoon to weave cloth?"

"Every week," Harold Junior said. "But you must not tell anybody."

"But uh . . . why not?" I asked. "After all, people are saying you are meeting with drug lords."

"Let them say what they will," Harold Junior said. "I prefer that they think that rather than know I am doing anything as sissy as spinning and weaving. It would ruin my macho image."

"Oh," I responded. "I see what you mean."

"Then you won't print it in the newspaper?" the sheriff asked.

I thought about his request for a second or two. This rumor-busting story would be a hard one for an editor to sit on, but even a public official like a sheriff must have some right to privacy.

"Okay, sheriff," I smiled. "This one's on me. The people of the county must always read the truth, but I don't suppose they have to read everything that's true."

INVENTING THE CUCUMTALOUPE

When your particular con is the country newspaper business, you are unlikely to be a man of wealth.

And most of my family-raising years, I struggled to retain my lofty status of lower middle class.

A little "found money" would have helped, but with the newspaper consuming 60 to 70 hours a week and 139 percent of my energy, a second job could be only a weak breakfast table joke.

To provide a bit more for my family than the newspaper was able to throw off, I decided to return to my farm roots and raise a garden. With the benefit of hindsight, it is clear that I should have known better.

Despite being "raised up" on a farm and being my mother's gardening assistant through early childhood, I had no aptitude for growing anything which required more grooming than athlete's foot fungus.

But I was determined to take the pressure off the family grocery bill by spading up half the back yard. I shoved the bedding plants into the ground, much as I had seen my mother do. After all, she had provided vegetables for us to eat until my boyhood eyes could no longer stand to see another black-eyed pea on my plate.

For my adult garden, there was one mistake I knew, from youthful experience, not to make.

One spring when my mother was pregnant with my youngest sister, she felt too asthmatic to plant the family garden, so as the oldest son, I took over the role of vegetable provider. Since I obviously already knew everything, I sought advice from no one as I planted what the family needed from tomatoes to okra. I went light on the vegetables I hated, but I devoted the entire north end of the garden to the plant I loved most: Watermelon.

I view cucumbers as no more than plate decoration, but my mother and grandmother loved to pickle them with smells that drove me out of the house and into the summer afternoon heat. I knew the garden wouldn't be a success in their eyes unless I grew them. So beside the five rows of watermelons, I planted one lone row of cucumbers.

Unlike my mother's earthen beds which prospered as if God himself were tilling them, my garden floundered. The insects got the tomatoes. The heat beat back the beans. And I mistook the okra for weeds and pulled it all up.

As summer progressed, I was left with only the garden's north side to show for my efforts. The cucumbers were thriving. For some reason known only to nature, cucumbers always thrive, and I am truly astounded that they have not yet taken over the world. My one cucumber row was growing southward, where the radishes and celery should have been, like some kind of science fiction plant. Grandmother could pickle her way into paradise.

But even better, the rows of watermelon plants on the far north side grew green and strong, and I had visions of summer watermelon delight every evening.

As I watched the melons grow bigger and more beautiful, their success overshadowed the failure of the remainder of the garden. I thumped them twice a day until one Saturday afternoon, I deemed that the biggest melon had ripened. I called my father, and he gave the melon one of his especially big thumb thumps. He, too, agreed it was time to eat.

With an immensity of pride which could only be conjured up by a 12-year-old, I picked the chosen watermelon and carried it to the back porch of the family farm house. I put it in the shade, placed a towel carefully over it, and cooled it with the runoff hose drippings of the evaporative cooler.

After supper, my father announced that, thanks to his brilliant oldest son, the family could have sweet melons for dessert, not only that evening but every summer evening we wanted if the size of that part of the watermelon garden was any indication.

My younger siblings stared at me with unaccustomed respect as they carried their plates and spoons and salt shakers onto the back porch. I felt like the Great Provider as I removed the cooling towel from the big watermelon and carried it to the top step where the family gathered with mouthwatering anticipation. My shirt pushed at its buttons as my father poised the long carving knife above my melon, and with the proper splitting sound of readiness, the watermelon was sliced open.

To my horror, the inside of the watermelon was not red as I had expected. It was a kind of off-green color.

"Why isn't it red?" My slightly young sister instantly picked out the flaw.

"Perhaps," my father said encouragingly, "it will taste good anyway."

The braver of us took bites, but these were quickly spat onto the ground.

"It tastes like cucumber," my slightly younger sister complained, and even though I would never admit it, she was right.

The family went back inside the house without the expected watermelon dessert, and I downtroddenly was left to figure out what went wrong.

The old farmer across the creek put his finger right on the problem with his first question to me: "You weren't stupid enough to plant the watermelon and the cucumber side by side, were you?"

"Well, I did plant them pretty close," I was forced to admit.

"They have cross-pollinated," he allowed. "What you have raised there, boy, is a 'watercumber,' or maybe it should be called a 'cucum-melon.' Don't fret. You haven't wasted your effort. The cows will love them."

Against this backdrop of failure, I launched into my adult garden. I was again the family farming provider. But I had no intention of making the same mistake twice. I planted the watermelon on one side of the backyard, and I planted the cucumbers on the far side, over by the cantaloupes.

And once again, I was beset by a series of plagues which even Moses would not have called down upon the Egyptians. The root rot got all of my stalk plants. The deer ate my beans and watermelon. The rabbits ate all the leafy stuff, and the heat and insects got all the rest.

All, of course, except for the cucumbers, which had prospered and were taking over much of the yard. Even the grass seemed in retreat. And to my delicious delight, the cataloupe plants were also doing fine. My family would at least have some tasty cataloupe to brighten our meals.

But when we cut into the first cantaloupe, a vision of deja vu flashed before my eyes. The humiliation of my youth came back in waves as I looked at a cantaloupe which was not a deep yellow in color but a rather pale greenish shade.

It was, one might say, a "cucumtalope."

Or perhaps it was a "cantacumber."

Cows liked it.

THE NIGHT I DIDN'T SPEND IN THE RED LIGHT DISTRICT

What is the most important freedom in America?
When asked that question, the majority of Americans answer that the most important is freedom of religion. Others say freedom of speech.
But I have come to conclude that the most basic, essential freedom upon which the others can be assembled and maintained is economic freedom.
While attending a state university in the 1960s, I was taught not to think that way, and I went out into the newspaper world with a feeling of guilt because the newspaper was a business and not pure public service. I apologized for the newspaper making a profit.
Slowly, I began to realize that freedom of speech and religion can truly exist only where there is economic freedom as the foundation. Newspapers in the United States are free because they make a profit and are not beholden to government or anyone except their customers, who vote for individual newspapers with their dollars.
An interesting contrast in "somewhat free" is Mexico.
For four years in my newspaper career, I viewed Mexico from a perfect vantage point: Three miles away. I was privileged to be the publisher and part owner of a small daily newspaper on the border with Mexico in the late 1970s. The downtown on the U.S. side of the border was three short miles to the downtown on the much more populous but commercially smaller Mexican side. Across the border was

a daily newspaper, two weekly newspapers, several magazines, and assorted other media.

My newspaper was probably the smallest in the U.S. with an international bureau, which consisted of Tony the taxi driver who fed us daily dispatches in Spanish about the routinely bizarre happenings in a Mexican border town. These hand-carried news notes were translated by Felipe, our ace Mexican-American reporter, into something that made some semblance of sense to those of us on the American side. On a day-to-day basis, Tony proved a reliable source of reasonably accurate news, but when there was a governmental trouble in the border town, Tony went "esconder," or into hiding, and Felipe had to cross the border and report for us. Tony knew better than to write about government corruption or a coup d'état, even at the municipal level.

As I struggled to learn how the Mexican system worked, I asked Felipe: "Is there no freedom of the press in Mexico?"

"Oh yes," Felipe responded. "There is absolute freedom of the press in Mexico." And he presented me with a partial copy of the Mexican constitution to prove it.

The U.S. constitution makes only a fleeting reference to freedom of speech and the press, which is the familiar "Congress shall pass no law . . ." portion. On the other hand, the constitution of Mexico spewed page after page of specific guarantees of press freedom. If you looked only at the two documents, your conclusion would be that while the U.S. press might enjoy some freedom from Congress, the Mexican press would be much more free with thousands of words to protect its right to print.

"So why can't the press in Mexico say whatever it wants?" I asked Felipe. "The constitution repeatedly and adamantly declares that freedom of the press is absolute."

"You will find out this afternoon," Felipe said with a smile. "I just received a telephone call from the publisher of *The Zocalo*. He desperately wants to see you right away."

Relatively new in town, I had not yet met my peer and, to some extent, my competitor from across the border, but I had heard that the publisher of *The Zocalo* came from a distinguished and courageous Northern Mexico newspaper publishing family. I could not imagine what he could want from me.

When he arrived at my office, he very properly introduced himself as Alfredo. Obviously a man of the aristocracy, Alfredo said that, in the name of freedom of the press, he came to ask for one thing: Newsprint.

"Newsprint?" I failed to recognize immediately how supplies were a freedom of the press issue. What a dummy I was. "Why are you short of newsprint?"

"We have no newsprint," Alfredo patiently explained, "because we wrote a series of editorials critical of the government last month."

"But I've looked at the Mexican constitution, and it clearly states that your newspaper can say anything about the government that it wants."

"Yes, that is true. *The Zocalo* can say anything it wants," Alfredo admitted, "but the government owns all the newsprint manufacturing and distribution in Mexico, and it can sell newsprint to whichever newspaper it wants. Since we wrote those editorials, it no longer wants to sell newsprint to *The Zocalo*. No newsprint, no freedom of the press."

"No newspaper," I now understood.

In the late 1970s, newsprint was in short supply as demand exceeded supply. One of the major Canadian mills was on strike which made the situation even worse, and I wasn't certain I would be able to obtain all the newsprint I needed that year. But Alfredo must acquire a couple of tons just to stay in business for the next few weeks, so I gambled and loaned him four full rolls.

Alfredo was genuinely grateful. He vowed to replace the newsprint as soon as he could, and he did some weeks later. In the meantime, word travels as fast as the clip of the tongue in a Mexican border town. Soon, both weekly newspaper publishers were in my office pleading for newsprint end rolls (the difficult-to-use portion of a roll of paper which is closest to the core) to keep putting out their publications, which also opposed the government in the same local issue.

Unable to silence the press by withholding newsprint, the government eventually had to make some concessions to the leaders of the border town, and in the Mexican fashion, things settled back down. But this time for a change, the local press had prevailed.

And as for me, I was learning why economic freedom is the building block for all freedoms. But I had much to learn about the culture only three miles away.

A few weeks later, Felipe came into my office and sat down.

"Boss," he said, "the Sociedad de Periodistas (the Society of Journalists) want to honor you for being a friend to the Mexican newspapers. The society has invited you to speak to their group on Thursday night."

"Uh, uh . . . uh," I muttered, "Felipe, you have heard my Spanish. I can't talk to a group of journalists. They would laugh themselves under the table."

"Just prepare a few general remarks," Felipe encouraged me. "Four or five minutes will be plenty. They will appreciate the attempt, however lame. I always go to their gatherings, and I will take you with me. I will jump in if you get bogged down in the language. For an American to be asked to speak is a great honor, and it is really good for international relations."

"Oh, all right. I'll do my best. What time should I meet you here at the newspaper on Thursday evening? Six o'clock?"

"No," Felipe said, "let's meet about nine."

"Nine o'clock at night to leave for the meeting? Felipe, you know the editor is off this Friday, and I will have to run the desk that day. That means I must arrive by five in the morning. I can't be up too late. I haven't put the paper out here before."

"But boss," Felipe said, "there's no point in leaving before nine. The meeting doesn't start until ten."

"The meeting doesn't even start until ten o'clock at night? What time will it be over?"

Felipe thought for a moment. Then he dodged a direct answer: "Oh, once it begins, it won't take long."

For the next few evenings, I put my Spanish dictionary at my elbow and carefully crafted a five-minute address for the Sociedad de Periodistas. I knew enough about Mexico to understand how highly regarded is the orator who can speak in the flowery, formal high Spanish. Such a person is much in demand. I would be lucky to speak in any sort of Spanish, but I wrote the best speech I could and rehearsed it endlessly. I took my wife out to an early dinner on that Thursday night, but I didn't eat since I would be dining with the Sociedad later that evening.

"Honey, this meeting doesn't even start until ten o'clock, so I may not be at home until 11:30 or maybe even midnight," I warned.

Felipe and I climbed in his low-riding Chevrolet at the newspaper and drove the three miles across the border into Mexico. When we arrived at the stucco building with outside staircase leading to the upstairs room where the society was to meet, the door was closed and still padlocked.

"It's too early," Felipe explained. "Let's go to Papagayo Bar and have a beer until the journalists begin to arrive."

Papagayo Bar was down the block and around the corner on a side street from the center of town. It was one of those campesino bars where the working men of Mexico congregated and washed down a day's worth of the ever-present border town dust. When we walked through the door, the friendly Felipe was hailed by everyone in the bar, and soon we had bought one round of those wonderful

Mexican beers and had two more bought for us. Felipe went to check once to see if any members of the Sociedad had arrived, but the padlock was still in place. We bought another round.

"Felipe," I tugged at his elbow, "it's 10:15. Time to go to the meeting."

"Naw,' he pushed me away. "Those journalists won't be there yet. Let's have another cerveza."

We did, and yet another. As the hour neared 11:00, I slipped away from the happy Felipe and went to check the building where the meeting was to be held. To my relief, the door was unlocked at last. I hustled up the steps to find a janitor sweeping out the meeting room all by himself.

"At what hour gathers the Sociedad de Periodistas?" I asked in Spanish.

"Pronto (soon), presto, luego," he answered looking at his watch. Then he guessed midnight or midnight thirty.

Midnight before the meeting even began? I went back to Papagayo Bar where the multi-talented Felipe was doing coin tricks for his adoring fans.

"Felipe," I tried to interrupt, "just how long is this meeting of the Sociedad going to take?"

"It won't take long," he assured me as he flipped a peso spinning atop the bar, "once it begins. Have another beer."

I did, and yet another. Midnight passed with no break in the Papagayo festivities. I bit my tongue and tried very hard not to be the stereotypical Norteamericano who has the bad manners in laid-back Mexico to insist that things happen on time. As I despaired of seeing the start of the Sociedad meeting, a group of Mexican journalists came through the door, performed the Mexican handshake with Felipe, and smiled at me. To my relief, they drank only one beer before escorting us to the meeting.

"At last," I thought, "we can get this thing going. I might still make it home before 2:00."

A number of journalists had gathered around the Carta

Blanca keg, the center of the social activity, and they handed me still another beer. I was already four over my limit, but they were such gracious hosts I could not refuse.

The next time I checked my watch, it was two beers and another hour later. The meeting room was now full of media type people, and the dinner was being laid out and would clearly be served sometime after 2:00 in the morning.

"Felipe," I pulled him aside. "Just how much longer is this going to last?"

Felipe, now fully immersed in spreading goodwill between the U.S. and Mexico, gave the answer I cringingly had come to expect: "It won't take long . . . once it begins."

After dinner, a street mariachi band performed several numbers, and someone's daughter sang five or six songs for the appreciative Sociedad while the journalists attacked the beer keg with determination.

Finally, the speeches began, and Felipe leaned over to me at 3:00 in the morning and whispered, "It won't take long now."

Weary and beginning to slur even my English words from too much beer, I suddenly caught the drift of the seventh speaker. He was talking about me. The time for the presentation and my speech must be close.

When the speaker completed his ornate introduction of me, I stood and staggered towards the podium to accept the honorary membership in the Sociedad which was being given me. I had consumed far too much beer before adding any food to my bloodstream, and it was all I could do to remain on my feet when he turned the speaker's stand over to me. It was sometime after three in the morning when I steadied myself against the stand, and with inhibitions subdued by alcohol, I launched into my prepared Spanish text on the serious subject of freedom of the press in a loud and confident voice.

But if I was a bit blurred, my audience also was a watercolor in the rain. It laughed and clapped and cheered at every broken sentence, so I felt free to ad lib at will, even where probably most inappropriate. If it had been a stand-up comedy club, I would have risen to the rank of headliner that night.

When I had completed my prepared text and rambled in unprepared territory for another four or five minutes, I mustered the good sense to tuck my honorary membership under my arm and sit back down.

"How long Felipe?" I moaned.

"It won't be long now," he gaily answered.

For a few moments, I slumped in my chair. Then I gritted my teeth and checked my wrist watch: 4:00 in the morning! I had my award. I had made my speech. I could go back to the U.S.

"Felipe, I have to be at work in an hour. I'm going if I have to crawl back across the border."

Felipe reluctantly consented to drive me, and he stood up to say good night to his friends. To my dismay, several of them requested rides home in Felipe's car, and the good-natured reporter turned none of them down. We packed his Chevrolet full of drunken journalists like it was a college telephone booth and delivered them to the back streets and far corners of the border town. At 5:00 in the morning, Felipe and I crossed back to the American side. I was already late to begin my work on the newspaper's desk, but I had to have a shower before I could begin pulling the wire, making assignments, and organizing that day's edition.

When I reached my house, all lights were on, and a most angry wife patted her foot on the floor: "Where have you been?"

"You are not going to believe . . ."

"I believe. You've spent the night over in the red light district, haven't you?"

"I wish I had," I answered, "I'd certainly be in better shape to put out today's newspaper."

Somehow, mostly by rote, I managed to get that Friday newspaper on the streets, although that particular edition did not turn out a triumph of great publishing.

I felt miserable for a couple of days, and yet that honorary membership from the Sociedad de Periodistas hangs on my wall as one of my most cherished possessions. In time, I came to respect the Mexican way of doing things through the puzzlement of a one-party democracy. It was not the Norteamericano style, but it had many of the balance-of-power elements necessary to provide a large degree of economic freedom and stability in an underdeveloped land. To this day, I love Mexico and its people, and I never miss an opportunity to visit.

But as for my wife, she suspected that I had spent the night in the border town's Zona Rojo (red-light district) until four months later when she accompanied me to a formal dinner on the Mexican side which, to her chagrin, did not even start until almost midnight, four hours late, and did not wind up until far past 2:00.

When we arrived home at 3:00 in the morning, she smiled and said, "I'm sorry."

"Those Mexican fetes don't take long," I said with the authority of an expert, "once they begin."

FAITH AND THE FLASHBULB

A weakness of late 20th Century man is that he has come to believe in technology.

Without having to erect even one church, technology has been elevated almost to the status of religion, an unchallenged tenet of which is this: A technological gadget can do anything.

Small-town newspapers are rarely the leaders in the unerring march of "progress," and my newspaper lags along the tail end of any advance. I embrace a new process only when it becomes impossible to operate without it . . . and only two weeks before that technology is officially obsolete.

Early in my newspaper career, I became suspicious of electronic creations. I discovered an uncorrectable flaw in the faith of my fellow man through his unshakable belief in a little marvel of wizardry that was called the peanut flashbulb (now made obsolete, of course, by the same God Technology which created it).

Named for its size, the peanut flashbulb was plugged in atop the cameras of its day. The only thing big about the peanut flashbulb was the faith that the camera's owner placed in it.

For those of us who are trying hard to forget our high school physics, a flashbulb ejects a burst of light for a fraction of a second. To make an image on the film, this light must strike an object and bounce back through the lens of the camera in sufficient quantity to record its target.

The limitation is that light diffuses very quickly, and that fact of physics makes a peanut flashbulb have a limited range of ten or twelve feet, or to stretch it, maybe fifteen feet. Beyond about twenty feet, the light is so diffused that a peanut flashbulb helps not at all.

But try to explain that to the many believers in the power of the flashbulb.

When the Astrodome first opened in Houston, I dutifully made my pilgramage to technology's newest shrine along with tens of thousands of others to see the first series of indoor baseball games, which by the way, were almost rained out. The builders of the Astrodome did not realize that they would be forced to air condition the giant indoor stadium 24 hours a day, 365 days a year. However, when the air conditioning was turned off, Houston's humidity caused a big cloud to form in the top of the dome, and it began to rain.

The first games had another technological glitch. The glare from the transparent roof made catching even the simplest of fly balls impossible for the outfielders. Astrodome officials tried painting the baseballs orange, but the glare still turned every pop-up into a single. Then they attempted painting the ceiling black to cover an area behind home plate, but that still didn't solve the problem. Eventually, they had to paint the entire dome ceiling black, and, of course, the grass died. Thus, necessity being the mother of invention, Astroturf was born.

But I digress. As a poor journalist, the best seat I could afford was high up in center field. I was escorted to my distant perch by one of the cute little Astro-hostesses in a skimpy space uniform. When I sat down, I noticed right away that all across the Astrodome people were pointing their little Kodaks at the vast expanse and taking pictures illuminated by their peanut flashbulbs. Everywhere I looked there was a wonderland of pop . . . pop . . . pop . . . pop . . . pop. . . .

The fellow seated beside me took his camera, plugged in his peanut flashbulbs and proceeded to join the thousands of flashbulb enthusiasts: Pop . . . pop . . . pop . . . pop. . . .

After he had gone through a role of film and had started on a second, I foolishly decided to help the misguided guy. I informed him that a peanut flashbulb would do him no good if he wanted to take a picture of home plate, some 450 feet away from us if it was an inch.

He pointed to the pop . . . pop . . . popping which was going on all over the stadium. "You mean all these people are wasting their film," he said in disbelief as his wife leaned over to listen in.

"Completely," I replied.

But he wouldn't take my word for it. He called to the nearest Astro-hostess and asked her. The response still echoes in my head: "Oh yes sir, use your flashbulbs. We find people get a lot better results taking pictures of the Astrodome with their flashbulbs."

The man at my elbow looked at me as if to say, "So there," and he shot up another two roles of film: Pop . . . pop . . . pop toward the action a telescope's view away.

I had been put in my place, but I would have loved to know what his wife said when the man's film came back from the store.

The most poignant example of this faith in the flashbulb came early one evening when a telephone caller requested a word with the newspaper's photographer. So I pulled him out of the black cave which is sometimes called a darkroom.

When he ended his phone conversation, the photographer began to laugh without control or restraint. After a minute or two, he was able to talk again. The call, it seems, came from a woman who asked: "I want to take a picture of the moon tonight. How big a flashbulb will I need?"

The photographer responded: "Lady, if you could put at atomic blast on the top of your camera, you still wouldn't have enough."

But we all know she didn't listen. She was out there firing away at the moon with her peanut flashbulbs. Pop . . . pop . . . pop . . . pop. . . .

POISONING IN PAPA DOC'S PARADISE

My major weakness as a journalist is that I don't like to rock the boat.

Oh, I can delight in shaking up the stuffy establishment. But quite literally, I don't like the boat to rock at all. Or the airplane. Or the train. Or the bus.

In short, I am one of those people who suffer from motion sickness.

I am the only person I ever knew who was already hanging over the rail of a ship on the English Channel before it had even left the dock at Calais. By the time I reached Dover, I understood why the British Isles have been invaded so rarely. If Adolf Hitler had landed an Army that felt like I did when I finally hugged the solid ground of North Downs, a handful of British housewives could have swept the Nazis back into that meanest of seas.

This motion malady may be the strongest single reason why, as a young man, I chose community newspapering over an attempt to reach for the pinnacle of big-time journalism. Whenever I thought how glamorous working for *Time* magazine might be, I reminded myself that the editors of *Time* would probably expect one of its staffers to be willing to get on a jet and fly wherever the story might demand. Better for me if the story demands a journey no further than White's Feed Store.

But of course, a journalist infected with terminal motion sickness knows one thing for certain: Whenever a story comes up which requires a tumultuous trip of any kind, he will be assigned to cover it.

Guess who white-knuckled his way onto almost every mountain top in Korea to do a brass-initiated story on the ever-vigilant but always ignored missile command for *Pacific Stars and Stripes*.

Guess who existed for weeks on a deck-boat cot while a Philippine freighter, which would make that slow boat to China look fast, wandered through the scores of islands between Cebu and Mindanao before foolishly turning out into the Sulu Sea to be caught in the season's worst typhoon. And amid much laughter from his fellow Filipino passengers, guess who had to hurl his favorite straw hat into the San Bernardino Strait while crossing between the islands of Samar and Luzon because the tiny boat had no other container.

Guess who was always volunteered in Vietnam to climb into the back of any helicopter or into the steaming sauna cargo-hold of any C-series transport plane to head for some remote jungle outfit deemed in need of recognition.

Guess who was selected to fly for a week with the one-engine mail plane from station to station (ranch to isolated ranch) across the vast Queensland and Northern Territory of the Australian outback seated beside a bush pilot who insisted I lift my head enough to help him search for the barren spots he considered landing strips.

So it should have been no surprise when the editor called me into his office one afternoon and assigned me to depart at 6 a.m. the following day on a plane bound for Haiti. Another staffer had previously covered the story, but he quite rationally refused to climb aboard an old DC-3 and set out for the Caribbean for three days of fearful flying. While I hated the thought of subjecting myself to certain motion sickness again, the story was irresistible.

A former car dealer and banker named Don Pierson in the little town 30 miles to the east had always been a remarkable promoter, but in recent years, he had turned into an extraordinary player on the international scene. With a confidence born of dominating the minor leagues, Pierson steamed into the majors by boldly purchasing a mothballed American warship and stationing it in the North Sea just outside the territorial limits of England for some offshore broadcasting into London. Pierson would make a mint by circumventing the government in the lucrative but overcontrolled London broadcast market.

That a southern small town car dealer and banker would have the pluck even to attempt such a defiance of Great Britain attracted worldwide press coverage, but just when it appeared Pierson might make a profit from his gutsy venture, the British Parliament passed a new law which extended the nation's jurisdiction over its waters and destroyed Pierson's broadcasting plans.

Pierson found himself stuck with an aged warship. The U.S. Navy was not about to take it back, and the supply of mothballed navy vessels far exceeded world demand. Operating the ship was now costing him many thousands of dollars a day with no end to the cash drain in sight. One might have thought Pierson stuck in financial ruin, but anyone who can unload an entire floor plan of new automobiles in a little town before the turn of the model year can find a way to deal one worn-out warship.

With unerring salesmanship, Pierson located the one man on earth who was in the market for the prestige of a warship: Francois "Papa Doc" Duvalier, the dictator of Haiti. Papa Doc had always longed to have a Haitian Navy, and Pierson's outlandish vessel could be his flagship, indeed his only ship of any significance. Never mind that it was so obsolete that it would not frighten even tiny Barbuda, the warship would look impressive sitting in the harbor at Port-Au-Prince, and this might intimidate the people Papa Doc most wanted to scare away: His own subjects. Somehow, Haiti was trying to prepare for "boat people" two decades before Americans realized they were coming. So Papa Doc negotiated for Pierson's floating white elephant.

Alas, Haiti had no money, not even enough to buy an obsolete warship, so Pierson eventually had to unload the ship for its scrap-iron value, but the talks with Papa Doc produced something Pierson believed would prove even more lucrative than offshore broadcasting in England. Pierson negotiated a 99-year lease for the rights to develop a free port on the Island of Tortuga, a pristine shell of land 25 miles long and five miles wide located some ten miles north of Haiti.

However, luck was not on Pierson's side. Papa Doc, the voodoo cultist who had just decided to reopen Haiti after two decades of shutting it off from the rest of the world, had the bad timing to die, and the family dictatorship passed on to the much less capable hands of his son, Jean-Claude "Baby Doc" Duvalier.

With a coup d'état being attempted every couple of months, Pierson desperately wanted to launch his Tortuga development and stabilize at least his part of the country, but investors are reluctant to sink money in a nation where the collapse of the government could come with any radio bulletin. In the Baby Doc power vacuum, spreading the bribes around fast and deep enough to keep the Tortuga lease intact for even nine months, much less 99 years, took all of Pierson's considerable skills. Pierson needed publicity for his project to convince the financial world Haiti was safe for the millions in investment required. If dollars began raining on Haiti, perhaps there would be enough to satisfy even the most corrupt of all Western Hemisphere "governments."

In handing me the assignment, my editor said that Pierson's staff had told him that *The New York Times*, *The Wall Street Journal*, and the Associated Press had also agreed to send writers along on the flight to Haiti, and he didn't want us to be scooped by *The New York Times* in our own backyard. Our newspaper must have a reporter on the trip.

At dawn on an early autumn day, I drove up to the cropduster airport where Pierson's World War II surplus DC-3 sat poised to take to the skies. Not surprisingly, the promised national press did not arrive, leaving me the lone media representative on what had been billed as a public relations flight. Other seats were filled by a couple of bankers and the town's mayor who sat back in the remodeled executive-style of the overly vintaged airplane and admired the politically astute three-foot portrait of Baby Doc on the door to the cockpit.

To my amazement, the plane would fly. Without incident, we took to the skies, flew across the southern part of the United States, and landed in Miami to refuel; then we flew parallel to the coast of Cuba across the Atlantic Ocean towards Port-Au-Prince, the capital of Haiti. The afternoon's rising heat made the air bumpy, and the other passengers amused themselves with my queasiness.

However, everyone became squeamish when Pilot Al came back sweating into the passenger compartment and, with a miserable attempt at sounding casual, announced that a headwind might prevent the plane from reaching Port-Au-Prince before dark. The runway at the Port-Au-Prince airport had minimal lighting, but Haiti was such a poor country that the lights were not turned on unless arrangements were made in advance to land after dark.

"You mean, we are going to arrive at Port-Au-Prince after dark, and there will be no lights on the runway?" the mayor wanted to know. "How can we land?"

"We can't." Pilot Al, his face unable to hide his own concern, confessed: "If we can get close enough to radio the control tower before it closes for the night, we can have the lights turned on. Otherwise . . ."

"Otherwise what?" the mayor asked.

"Otherwise," the pilot shook his head sadly, "we'll have to fly somewhere else."

"What somewhere else? The Bahamas?"

"No," Pilot Al said. "We only have enough fuel to go either back to Cuba or to Santo Domingo in the Dominican Republic. And for political reasons, Cuba is out. It will have to be Santo Domingo."

"But do they have runway lights turned on in Santo Domingo?"

"I think so," Pilot Al said, "but we are forbidden to land there. If we have to put down in the Dominican Republic, we will probably be retained there for several weeks."

For an anxious hour, we watched as the dark curled around the edge of the eastern horizon and twilight retreated in the west. But almost simultaneously with one of the bankers collapsing in fear, Pilot Al announced that Co-Pilot Bill had made contact with the Port-Au-Prince airport, and the runway lights would be turned on for us.

After 12 hours in the air, we landed and, with instructions to skip customs, climbed into taxis for harrowing rides into the capital city and rooms at the only hotel of semi-western standards. While the rest of the recovering party planned dinner in the hotel dining room, I wanted to take to the teeming Iron Market of Haiti for food and adventure.

"You'd better not eat with the locals" the pilot warned. "You will get sick for sure."

However, I had traveled the globe eating from the local economy without negative consequences. To the horror of my medical friends, I often journeyed to Mexico and ate with the street vendors just to keep my intestinal system in the toughest possible shape. I was not about to miss the chance to taste authentic Haitian food. While they dined in the pretend Hilton, I walked among the colorful people of Haiti, somehow cheerful amid some of the worst poverty I had ever seen. The Iron Market filled the senses with everything Haitian, even though the market was mostly closed for the night by the time I arrived. Women who lived on their retail sales space hurried to respread their wares when they saw the lone tourist coming.

The street vendors cooked foods with most unusual smells, and some of it seemed inviting to my stomach, now hungry and recovering from the emptying it received during the flight. But as a matter of prudence, I selected a small restaurant not too far from the Iron Market and ate what my schoolboy French could tell them to bring me from the menu. I think it was a rice and chicken dish of some kind. I never knew for certain. The seasoning reminded me of something Lebanese, and while I wouldn't consider it five star, the meal was delightful and generally filling.

"Oh boy, are you going to be sick," Pilot Al scolded me when I returned to the hotel. "Just wait until that flight tomorrow out to Tortuga. You will be turning inside out."

The following morning, we braved the taxis again, climbed back into the refueled DC-3 and took off for the Isle de la Tortue (Tortuga). The half hour flight took us over the fortress of Cap Haitien, imposing even from 10,000 feet, and to the little island which was named Tortuga by Columbus because he thought its flat ridges resembled a turtle. The island had its only moment in history when Columbus' flagship, the Santa Maria, sank off its coast.

We landed on a 4,000-foot strip which had been hacked out of the jungle by some of the island's 9,000 black residents using their machetes and the acid of orange juice to loosen the limestone. A dozen French-speaking natives rushed out of three thatched-roof huts to greet us. Once on the ground, the hot tropical sun and thick bush limited our movements. The east side of the island had only one short unpaved road and one ancient vehicle used to haul goods to the huts from a small inlet used as a harbor.

Pierson's lieutenants busily pointed out where this multi-million dollar motel will be located and where that world-class resort will be situated. Within a few months, they contended, Caribbean cruise ships will be stopping on these beaches with their white sand and emerald waters.

"This island is heaven," they stated without reservation, "and we will develop paradise right here."

But it was far from paradise yet. With no restaurant, no restroom, no facilities of any kind, our party only stayed on the end of the island for two hours before all agreed it was time to depart. We climbed back into the DC-3, whose wheels were now almost buried in soft sand, and plowed down the soft runway with the plane fighting the heated air for enough lift to clear the trees beyond the machete-hacked strip. By my reckoning, we soared above the palms with a couple of feet to spare.

Afternoon tropical heat currents transformed the flight back to Port-Au-Prince into an amusement park ride, and soon the plane's passengers turned as green as the Caribbean water below. Shortly later, Pilot Al stumbled back into the passenger area of the plane holding his stomach. The pilot threw himself down on the couch cushions and whispered that he was violently ill, as was Co-Pilot Bill. But he thought Co-Pilot Bill would be able to hold out long enough to land in Port-Au-Prince. With that, he collapsed prostrate on the executive couch unable to wiggle.

If ever there was an original motion sickness man, it was me. And yet as I viewed the forest of contorted faces inside the compartment, I suddenly realized that I was the only one on the airplane who was not sick. I had seen the movie where a non-pilot has to take the controls and be talked down by the radio tower, and the adrenal secretions from that thought replaced my unsettled stomach with unsettling fear. As I wondered if I could land the plane if necessary, Co-Pilot Bill managed to put it down at Port-Au-Prince before he, too, became incapacitated. The pilot and co-pilot had to be carried from the airplane, and taxis took the constantly vomiting group back to the hotel for an emergency visit from a Haitian doctor.

The doctor pronounced everyone else on the plane seriously ill with food poisoning. Since I was the only one who did not have this Papa Doc poisoning, it was obvious that they all got it from the hotel restaurant last night while I dined in a little restaurant near the Iron Market.

Gleefully, I telephoned my editor and informed him I would be stuck in Haiti for several more days while the pilot and co-pilot recovered from food poisoning. I enjoyed my unplanned vacation in Papa Doc's "paradise," but Haiti proved too corrupt and too unstable for international investment, and the Island of Tortuga remains much the way it was when Columbus first named it.

For dictators like Papa Doc and his successors, I suppose Haiti may have been their privileged private paradise. For their countrymen, the poor and corrupt island is much closer to hell.

A LITTLE ADVICE AT THIRTY

Journalists always ponder how to start things but rarely think about how to end anything.

It's an occupational hazard which comes from carefully crafting, what newspapermen call the 'lede,'' or the first paragraph of any story, and never giving any consideration to the last paragraph.

The lead paragraph, after all, is what hooks the reader into the story after he has gone for the bait of the headline. A short, punchy, story-telling opening paragraph is the hallmark of a good journalist, and some great "ledes" stand out in my mind even though the reporters who penned them have become blurred by time.

For example, our newspaper once sent a talented young writer to a neighboring town to cover a rattlesnake roundup sponsored by the Jaycees. In particular, we wanted him to write about his first taste of rattlesnake which was skinned and stinkingly deep-fried on the spot by the temporarily insane service club. When he came back, the opening paragraph of his story read:

"The problem with eating rattlesnake is that you always get the neck."

At times, one little fact in the "lede" of the story can help the reader visualize what really happened. Our reporter came back from covering an election which ended in a brawl and wrote this classic opening sentence:

"When attacked by two poll watchers minutes after the polls closed Saturday at the City Hall Voting Precinct, Election Judge Randall Thomas was severely handicapped in the early moments of the fight because he had a ballot box under each arm."

The story went on to say that, despite his slow start, the hefty election judge was able to polish the sidewalk's cement with the two poll watchers who no doubt wished they had filed their complaint with the state's attorney general instead.

In journalism, the "lede" is all-important. The opening paragraphs will be printed and will be read by subscribers.

But alas, the last paragraph of the story was likely to wind up in the hell bucket in the olden hot-type days or cut by scissors and left waxed to the composing room floor in more recent times. Newspapermen are taught to write in what is called, puzzlingly, the "inverted pyramid" style, which means that all of the important items go at the top of the story and the less essential details trail off at the end. That way, an editor can cut a story from the bottom to fit in a hole in the page without being concerned that he is dropping some vital detail. That way, the reader can glean the information he needs from the top part of the story and skip the rest if he is pressed for time or simply not that interested.

As a result, journalists often give little or no thought to the paragraph before the "30 dash," the traditional typesetting signal that a news story has ended. As I approached the final "30 dash" of these little tales of small-town newspapering, it occurred to me that perhaps I shouldn't let this book trail off like a news story.

So I searched my memory for some particularly inspiring smalltown incident which would reward those patient enough to persevere to the book's end with the courage to face their lives anew, and here it is:

Some years ago, I sat at the luncheon counter of a tiny cafe on a hot summer afternoon discussing local politics and the price of cows over a glass of iced tea.

Behind the counter stood the perpetually frowning owner of the establishment, a man whose reputation for fiscal conservatism was confirmed by the fact that he kept his packages of sugar next to the coffee urn on the back wall to discourage their use. He rationed those Imperial sugar packs as if it were still World War II.

The day was hot and likewise was the counter debate, so I asked the owner for a refill of ice tea, only my second glass.

Without bothering to hide his displeasure at having to provide refills of tea for which the tradition of the community and the competition down the street dictated that he could not charge extra, he whipped over the tea pitcher and slopped my glass full once again.

As he started to walk away, I politely asked: "Excuse me, could I have some more sugar?"

The cafe owner whirled around and glared as if I had just requested possession of his first born. He pointed at the bottom of my iced tea glass and stated with undisguised indignation: "Stir what you got."

I lifted up my glass and peered into the bottom. Sure enough, there was a layer of white. I stirred, and the tea was indeed sweeter, almost as sweet as if the cafe owner had been generous enough to provide me with an additional packet of sugar.

For a moment, I tried to force myself to flash with anger at the rude owner, but he was so in-character that I found I could only be amused by him.

Then I began to ponder what he said. Actually, I had to admit, that's pretty deep thinking. As a newspaperman who has earned his living selling advertising in little communities, I have often wished for a big new shopping center to make life easier.

And how many of us are always asking for that one

extra little packet of sugar to sweeten things up when what we should be doing is making the most of the resources we have already at hand?

Perhaps the cheap cafe owner was right. It's good advice:

"Stir what you got."